T0339650

Exploiting future uncertainty

First published 2010 by Gower Publishing

Published 2016 by Routledge
2 Park Square, Milton Park, Abingdon, Oxon OX14 4RN
711 Third Avenue, New York, NY 10017, USA

Routledge is an imprint of the Taylor & Francis Group, an informa business

British Library Cataloguing in Publication Data
Hillson, David, 1955-
  Exploiting future uncertainty : creating value from risk.
  1. Risk management. 2. Strategic planning.
  I. Title
  658.1'55-dc22

Library of Congress Control Number: 2010937248

ISBN 13: 978-1-4094-2341-6 (pbk)

Exploiting future uncertainty

CREATING VALUE FROM RISK

Dr David Hillson
The Risk Doctor

Routledge
Taylor & Francis Group

LONDON AND NEW YORK

Contents

Contents

Prologue

My first experience of applying a structured approach to managing risk came in 1985 when I was a young and inexperienced project manager and my boss called me into his office. "We've decided to introduce risk management to the company, and we're starting with you." It turned out that my project had been selected as a pilot for this new-fangled thing, to see if it could help us deliver value to our customers more successfully. But when I asked for some guidance I discovered that I was on my own. Although we'd decided to "do risk management", we didn't know how.

So began my long journey, which continues to this day, to find out what risk management is really all about. From my earliest experiments with the format and content of Risk Registers and reports, through discovering the intricacies of Monte Carlo simulation and influence diagrams, to today's frontiers of risk attitudes and enterprise risk management, it's been a roller coaster. One thing has sustained me: risk management works!

I've found that applying some basic concepts through a simple process with a few supporting tools and an understanding of human nature can make a huge difference between success or failure. And once I'd learned some of the tricks of the trade I wanted to pass them on to others. Starting with my colleagues in the same company, then working with small consultancies, and finally through establishing Risk Doctor as a global risk consultancy, my goal has always been to share insights and get as many people as possible benefiting from managing their own risk successfully.

Communication has always played a big part in this strategy. Speaking at conferences and seminars, writing books and articles, contributing to blogs and discussion boards, answering emails and web queries – I've used them all to get the message out as widely as possible. One of the most successful channels has been Risk Doctor Briefings, distributed freely to the opt-in Risk Doctor Network and available for free download from the Risk Doctor website in multiple languages. Each of these one-page articles focuses on a single topic, offering proven tips and hints for practical application, addressing issues that many people find confusing or difficult about risk management.

Risk Doctor Briefings represent a great resource, a repository of useful advice and information. Anyone can download a briefing from the Risk Doctor website and use it to improve their understanding of risk management. But in keeping with our communication goal to spread the word to as many people as possible, we've repackaged the content of Risk Doctor Briefings into this book. Organised by five key themes and arranged into a logical sequence, the body of knowledge contained in the briefings is presented here as a coherent whole for the first time.

This is not a textbook, covering every aspect of risk management comprehensively and exhaustively. It does however address most of the things that people frequently find hard about managing risk. Each section presents a clear explanation of an issue and offers practical ways of dealing with it.

There are several ways you can use this book. You can dip in and read a single section on a particular topic, since each section is self-contained and deals with one subject. Or you can read a whole chapter to get a broader view of a theme. Or use the index to find specific items. However you use it, the aim is the same. I offer these insights to help you understand the risks you face, to give you proven ways of addressing them, and to enable you to create value from risk.

Of course there is no guarantee that everything in this book will work in every situation. Some of the perspectives may be controversial and you might disagree with what you read. But I invite you to engage with the material, think about what it says, and try to apply it in your own setting. If it works, then do it again – and please tell someone else. But if it doesn't work, then don't do it again – and please tell me!

I take full responsibility for this book, recognising that the content reflects my own limited perspectives and partial understanding of this complex and fascinating topic. But several people have made the book possible and they deserve my thanks. Lesley Hussell of Editing Edge transformed a series of stand-alone briefings into a single coherent manuscript, creating a compelling easy-to-read narrative. Sam Farrow's design team made Lesley's manuscript look great and gave it that je-ne-sais-quoi polish. I'm grateful to both Lesley and Sam for their expertise and encouragement. The thousands of Risk Doctor Network members provided the motivation to write the original briefings, and their feedback and comments have helped me to refine my thoughts and learn new things. My professional colleagues have patiently discussed risk theory and practice with me, testing my ideas, putting me straight in some areas, and helping to shape my approach. We don't always agree but the exchange is fun! And finally I'm indebted to my wife Liz, who brings reality to bear on the risk world, with her unique blend of gracious good humour and insightful wisdom.

But really this book is for you, the reader. I hope you find it stimulating, provocative, useful and challenging. The future is uncertain but we can exploit that uncertainty to create value. Go for it!

David Hillson, The Risk Doctor
Petersfield, Hampshire, UK

Introduction

What's new?

Navigation, the mariner said,
Is the key to our success or doom
The winds and tides are unknown Brides
To our uncertain future's Groom.

So scan the skies with clear-sighted eyes
For signs of events to come
Allow leeway for the vagary
And set your course for home.

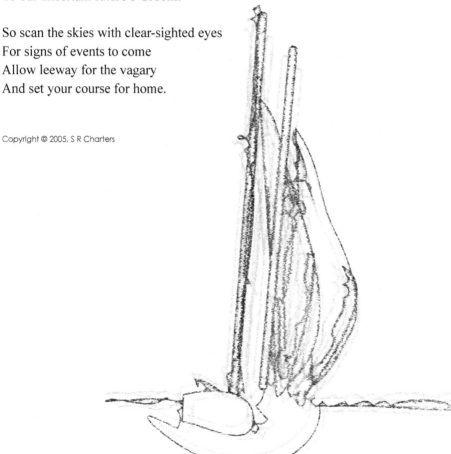

Picture a majestic galleon with billowing sails and a hopeful crew, tossed on stormy seas with the prospect of many perils ahead but also the lure of fabulous riches.

Humans have been dealing with risk for millennia, with more or less formality, and with greater or lesser degrees of success. In the Middle Ages when merchants set sail from Europe seeking their fortune in the East, they knew the journey would be fraught with danger. The potential for untold riches, however, led them to make the voyage despite the possibility of disaster. The old Italian word risicare (meaning "to dare" and the root of our modern word "risk") was used to describe the act of undertaking such an adventure, with two possible outcomes: sink and die or return fantastically wealthy.

The same concept of uncertainty included both downside and upside outcomes. Although only the negative sense of risk is common today, this book sets out to show how risk also means opportunity for every organisation. The Chinese concept of balance, expressed most commonly in yin yang, is used to describe many complementary opposites, including dark and light, female and male, low and high, cold and hot. The Chinese character wei ji is often translated as "risk" and has two elements that represent a similar duality (shown below), with one part meaning "danger" and the other meaning "opportunity."

If organisations wish to benefit from a broader view of risk, people will need to be re-educated in both thinking and language to ensure that both sides of risk as threat and opportunity are recognised and accepted. The Western cultural heritage which has produced the limited "risk = threat" formulation must be tackled head on.

The formal discipline called risk management offers a structured framework for identifying and managing risk. Given the prevalence and importance of the subject, we might expect risk management to be fully mature by now, only needing occasional minor tweaks and modifications to enhance its efficiency and performance. Surely there is nothing new to be said?

The Western cultural heritage which has produced the limited "risk = threat" formulation must be tackled head on.

While it is true that there is wide consensus on risk management basics, the continued failure of organisations to deliver consistent benefits suggests something is still missing. Clearly there must be some mismatch between risk management theory and practice, or new aspects to be discovered and implemented, otherwise all risks would be managed effectively and success would follow.

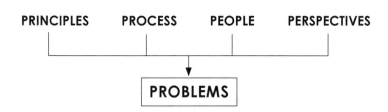

Here are some suggestions for how we might do things differently and better, under four headings:

1 **Principles**
2 **Process**
3 **People**
4 **Perspectives**

Problems with principles

There are two potential shortfalls in the way most organisations understand the concept of risk. The simplest way to describe risk is as "uncertainty that matters". Many people fail to see how this broad proto-definition of risk encompasses the idea that some risks might be positive, with potential upside impacts, mattering because they could enhance performance, save time or money, or increase value. As risks to objectives must be managed proactively, this should lead to the use of an integrated risk process to manage both threats and opportunities alongside each other. This maximises the chances of success by intentionally seeking out potential upsides and capturing as many as possible, as well as finding and avoiding downsides.

Another conceptual limitation is to think only about detailed low-level events or conditions when considering risk. This ignores risk to the organisation at a higher level, perhaps within a programme or portfolio, or perhaps in terms of delivering strategic value. The distinction between "overall risk" and "individual risks" is important, and if the higher-level connection is missing, the value that the risk process can deliver is limited. We will look at concepts in Chapter 2.

Problems with process

The risk process as implemented by many organisations is often flawed in a couple of important respects. The most significant of these is a failure to turn analysis into action, with Risk Registers and risk reports being produced and filed, but with these having little or no effect on how work is actually undertaken or how decisions are made. The absence of a formal process step to "Implement Risk Responses" reinforces this failing. Risk responses need to be treated in the same way as all other tasks, with an agreed owner, a budget and timeline, included in plans, reported on and reviewed. If risk responses are seen as "optional extras" they may not receive the degree of attention they deserve.

A second equally vital omission is the lack of a "Risk Lessons Learned Review" step in most risk processes. This is linked to the wider malaise of failure to identify lessons to be learned, denying the organisation the chance to benefit from experience and improve future performance. Such lessons include identifying which threats and opportunities arise frequently, finding which risk responses work and which do not, and understanding the level of effort typically required to manage risk effectively. We consider process in detail in Chapter 3.

The most significant process problem is a failure to turn analysis into action.

Problems with people

It is common for risk management to be viewed as a collection of tools and techniques supporting a structured system or a process, with a range of standard reports and outputs that feed into meetings and reviews. This perspective often takes no account of the human aspects of managing risk. Risk is managed by people, not by machines, robots or processes. We need to recognise the influence of human psychology on the risk process, particularly in the way risk attitudes affect judgement and behaviour. There are many sources of bias, both outward and hidden, affecting individuals and groups, and these need to be understood and managed proactively where possible.

The use of approaches based on emotional literacy to address the human behavioural aspects of managing risk is in its infancy, but some good progress has been made in principle and in practice. Without taking this into account, risk management is fatally flawed, relying on judgements made by people who are subject to a wide range of unseen influences, and whose perceptions may be unreliable – with unforeseeable consequences. The People Factor is the subject of Chapter 4.

> Risk is managed by people, not by machines, robots or processes.

Problems with perspectives

This book discusses risk management from the perspective of business and projects, but of course these are not the only areas where risk exists. We have much to learn from other risky endeavours, and this is addressed in Chapter 5. Here we can simply note that different people see risk in different ways. This arises from our definition of risk as "uncertainty that matters," and the fact that both the degree to which something is uncertain and the extent to which it matters is driven by perception. Given the same risky situation, different individuals, groups and organisations will see it differently. This can lead to a variety of reactions, from extreme caution to a desire to cast off restraint and take a chance. We should not limit our understanding of risk to our own perspective, but should instead seek to learn from the views of others. Much of the experience and wisdom of other people and groups can be transferred to our own situation if we are prepared to look outside our own limited perspective and consider how others see things.

So there is plenty new to be said about managing risk. Despite our long history in attempting to foresee the future and address risk proactively, we might do better by extending our concept of risk to include opportunity, addressing weak spots in the risk process, dealing with risk attitudes, and learning from how others approach the risks they face.

This practical book offers achievable ways to enhance the effectiveness of risk management, and might even help us to change the course of future history.

1

Risk Management and Better Business

THE LONG VIEW BACK

The earliest records of human history and prehistory include stories of risk and its management. If we take a long view back, we find historical documents, sacred writings, myths and legends – all telling tales of the human struggle against nature, the gods or the odds. Accounts of mankind's earliest origins describe the urge to break boundaries, to go beyond current confines, to explore the unknown.

Narratives describe risk-taking individuals ranging from Abraham, revered by three of the world's great religions for his faith in leaving home and setting out to find a new country, through mythological heroes like Jason or Odysseus who undertook epic journeys, to modern entrepreneurs and innovators who change the lives of millions through ground-breaking discoveries and inventions.

The world we inhabit is unpredictable, strange, incomprehensible, surprising, mysterious, awesome, different, other.

The broader sweep of human development has included risky phases as hunter-gatherers and agrarians, leading to the establishment of great civilisations like Egypt or the Mayans, to the present day.

Seen from a certain perspective, risk is everywhere. The world we inhabit is unpredictable, strange, incomprehensible, surprising, mysterious, awesome, different, other. This is true from the macro level of galaxies to the exotic nano-realm of subatomic particles, and everywhere in between. Irrefutable evidence forces people to accept the truth that we neither know nor understand everything, and we cannot control everything.

Consequently, the word "risk" has become a common and widely used part of today's vocabulary, relating to personal circumstances (health, pensions, insurance, investments etc), society (terrorism, economic performance, food safety etc), and business (corporate governance, strategy, business continuity etc).

And it seems that mankind has an insatiable desire to confront risk and attempt to manage it proactively. Many of the institutions of human society and culture could be viewed as frameworks constructed to address uncertainty, including politics, religion, philosophy, technology, laws, ethics and morality.

Each of these tries to impose structure on the world as it is experienced, limiting variation where that is possible, and explaining residual uncertainty where control is not feasible. Sense-making appears to be an innate human faculty, seeking patterns in apparent randomness. People apply a variety of approaches, both overtly and subconsciously, to reach an acceptable degree of comfort in the face of uncertainty.

> Many institutions of human society and culture could be viewed as frameworks constructed to address uncertainty, including politics, religion, philosophy, technology, laws, ethics and morality.

As a result, not only is risk everywhere, but so is risk management. Perhaps it is not too far-fetched to describe risk management as offering an integrative framework for understanding many parts of the human experience, if not all. Just as the presence of risk is recognised and accepted as inevitable and unavoidable in every field of human endeavour, so there is a matching drive to address risk as far as possible. This has led to a proliferation of areas where the phrase "risk management" is used to describe efforts to identify, understand and respond to risk, particularly in various aspects of business.

There seems little doubt that risk management has been part of human activity for a very long time, and it is today a vital component of business. As a result anyone asking the simple question, "What is risk management?" will not find a simple answer. Even the most cursory exploration reveals a huge variety of differing perspectives, all claiming to represent the best way to address risk.

In fact risk management is not a single subject at all; it is a family of related topics. These business applications range from project and technical risk management through operational and financial risk management up to strategic and enterprise-wide risk management. Other disciplines could also be included under the risk management umbrella, such as health and safety, business continuity, or corporate governance.

There are many common elements shared by these different types of risk management, but each has its own distinctive language, methodology, tools and techniques. They vary in scope from the broadest application to very specific areas of risk. They are at different levels of maturity, with some types of risk management being quite recent developments while others measure their history in decades or longer. But each is important in its own way, representing part of the response of business to the uncertain environment within which it operates.

All of this leads to one essential question: If risk is everywhere and risk management is so important, why don't we do it for our business? We are constantly confronted with business failures and in the rare cases where post-mortem reviews are held afterwards, causes of failure often include unforeseen-but-foreseeable risks.

Threats that should have been spotted and tackled turn into avoidable problems, and opportunities to create additional value or minimise waste and rework are missed. This continuing catalogue of failure indicates an ongoing lack of effective risk management. If we believe that our uncertain world can be managed proactively, then we need to find and address the missing critical success factors that are preventing risk management from delivering its promised benefits.

Mankind has always faced risk, from our earliest beginnings and throughout our history. Our survival and success as a species has largely resulted from our ability to understand and manage our uncertain environment, rising to each new challenge and adapting our behaviour to meet it. Perhaps we need to apply the same approach to how we manage the risks inherent in our business.

OPPORTUNITY KNOCKS

What is risk? And what impact does it have on your business? The simplest definition is that risk is **"an uncertainty that matters because it could affect your objectives."** The traditional position was that this referred always and only to negative things. After much hot debate, a new view has emerged.

Defining risk the old way, as "an uncertainty that could have an adverse effect leading to loss, harm or damage," limited the scope of the risk management process, which aims to avoid or minimise potential problems by acting proactively. It's true that by this yardstick traditional risk management has been very successful, and is now seen as a major contributor towards achieving business and project objectives.

However, using the risk process to deal only with the downside of uncertainty is an inevitable one-way street. If the process identifies only threats that could have an adverse effect, then responses designed to address these threats can only at best bring the performance back on target. It is much more likely that recovery of any deviation will be partial at best, leaving a shortfall in performance.

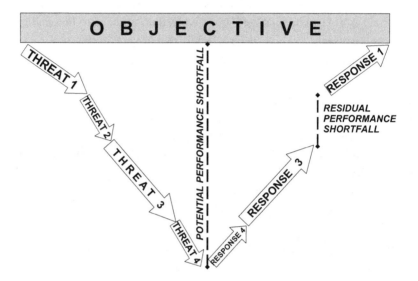

The realisation that threat-focused risk management only offers damage limitation has led to consideration of upside or positive risk – those uncertainties that could bring additional benefits if they were to occur – also known as "opportunities".

The definition of opportunity as **"an uncertainty that could have a positive effect leading to benefits or rewards"** is very similar to the traditional definition of "risk". In fact opportunity could be seen as just another form of risk: a risk with negative impacts is a threat, whereas a risk with a positive impact is an opportunity.

One side of the risk definition debate has concluded that risk should include both threat and opportunity, and that risk management should also address both types of uncertainty, seeking to minimise threats and maximise opportunities. This perspective is being reflected increasingly in risk management standards and professional guidelines, as well as in the practice of leading organisations.

So is opportunity just the flip side of threat? A standard examination question for medical students states, "Health is not the absence of disease: discuss." In the same way that peace is not the absence of war, or happiness is not the absence of sadness, it is also true that opportunity is not the absence of threat.

Of course, some opportunities are created when threats are removed (if staff do not take industrial action we could introduce an incentive scheme), and other opportunities are simply the inverse of related threats (instead of productivity being lower than planned, it might be higher). But there are also "pure opportunities" unrelated to threats: uncertain events or circumstances that would produce real additional benefits, if they could be captured proactively and exploited.

As well as identifying and addressing threats, it is equally important to seek and maximise opportunities, in order to optimise achievement of objectives: the opportunity to improve on your original plan by working "faster, smarter, cheaper" or the opportunity to reap significant unexpected rewards.

BETTER SAFE THAN SORRY? YOU CAN BE TOO CAREFUL

Whenever we face a risk, one of the biggest challenges is deciding what to do about it, if anything. This is not a simple matter. A wide range of influences affect how we respond to a risk. There are physiological factors relating to the "flight, fright or freeze" reaction. There are subconscious sources of bias arising from previous experience and internal frames of reference. And of course there are various measurable criteria that we can use to make a rational assessment of the situation.

One factor that is not often considered is the role of cultural norms of behaviour. These are often embodied in the popular sayings and proverbs that we all learn from our childhood. And while they often capture a great deal of learned wisdom and experience, some of these proverbs are misleading and can result in an inappropriate response.

In the context of managing risk, one of the most unhelpful sayings is the assurance that, "What you don't know can't hurt you." Many businessmen and project teams know only too well that this is far from the truth, and the archetypal unpredictable "Black Swan" events (popularised by Nassim Nicholas Taleb in his book "The Black Swan: The impact of the highly improbable") prove that unforeseen events can have a devastating impact if and when they happen.

Another proverb defines a common approach to managing risk that has shaped public and professional attitudes to risk in many ways. We've all heard the saying, "It's better to be safe than to be sorry." This sentiment has a more formal manifestation in a concept that affects a wide range of areas, including government policy, health and safety legislation, environmental standards, business regulatory frameworks, child protection practice, and even parenting guidelines. "Better safe than sorry" is also known as **the precautionary principle.**

The precautionary principle states that where there is a threat of severe or irreversible harm, and if there is no proof that harm would not result, it is better to take protective action. Decisions are then made to protect the public or the environment from the severe harm that might occur. Examples include reactions to the supposed but unproven "dangers" of genetically modified food, mobile phones or nanotechnology. We also hear tales of local authorities banning Christmas lights or hanging baskets "just in case" they fall on someone, or requiring schoolchildren to wear protective goggles when playing conkers.

The problem with the precautionary principle is that it leads to an over protective approach, wasting too much time and effort on things that might not ever be a problem. It can also lead the discipline of risk management into disrepute. When one of my friends learned I was a risk specialist, she got very cross about "silly rules at work" imposed by the "risk police" that mean she can't leave her handbag under her desk "just in case" someone trips on it.

The precautionary principle arises from a focus on one of the two main dimensions of risk to the detriment of another. It comes from concentrating on impact (what would happen if the risk occurred) but ignoring probability (how likely the risk is to occur at all). This is partly because the impact of a risk is easy to estimate or describe, whereas probability is a hard concept, especially where we have no relevant previous experience of this or a similar risk. We also discount probability because people generally are afraid of statistics. (Probability is a subject we will come back to in more detail in Chapter 3 of this book, which covers the practical application of the risk process.) But ultimately the precautionary principle simply reflects the "public wisdom" embodied in the proverb whereby we all know it is "Better to be safe than to be sorry."

How does the precautionary principle relate to business? We constantly encounter risks in all our projects and businesses, and many of these are novel with no previous history or track record to guide us in how to respond. As in public life, the temptation is to exercise caution, preferring safety "just in case", leading to an unnecessary overreaction to risks and a waste of valuable time and resources that could be better used elsewhere. Then when nothing happens and the risks that we all worried about never materialise, people say that risk management is just a lot of fuss about nothing.

In terms of public policy, the value of the precautionary principle is being challenged. A UK House of Lords enquiry even recommended that it should be dropped as an unhelpful influence, even though European law requires governments to take it into account when forming policy.

In business too, we should question whether "better safe than sorry" is the right approach. A few simple steps can help us to counter the tendency to be overprotective. For example:

- We should ensure that our risk process includes a realistic assessment of how likely a risk is to occur, as well as an estimate of its possible effect.
- We need to recognise that the worst-case level of impact almost never happens, and perhaps it would be better to develop responses that target the most likely impact.
- We must remember that some risks are good for us, and positive opportunities should be identified and pursued.
- We need to get used to ideas of "risk efficiency", balancing risk and reward, and accept that it is appropriate and necessary to take some risks.
- Finally we must improve our risk communication, being clear about exactly what risks we face, how likely they are to happen, what levels of impact could realistically result, and what responses are appropriate.

"Better safe than sorry" sounds like a good attitude to adopt, in life as well as in business. But it is possible to be too safe, being overprotective and cautious, preventing ourselves from taking the risks that are associated with progress, innovation and success. Let's banish the precautionary principle and use the risk process to ensure that we have no reason to be sorry.

RISK MANAGEMENT – IT'S NOT HARD

Daunted by the idea of mastering risk management because it looks "hard"? It doesn't have to be hard – in either sense of the word.

Firstly, many people assume risk management is difficult; some because they are afraid of statistics and think it is all about the use of arcane calculations. Perhaps we have painful memories of maths classes at school, or maybe we recall the words of Benjamin Disraeli when he referred to, "Lies, damned lies and statistics." Others believe it must be really difficult to imagine all the things that might happen in an uncertain future that might affect us.

> The risk process offers a structured way to think about risk, providing a framework to channel how we deal with risk intuitively.

Still others may have been put off by the fear of unmanageable "unknown unknowns", or confused by the somewhat garbled statement of Donald Rumsfeld in February 2002 that, "…as we know, there are known knowns; there are things we know we know. We also know there are known unknowns; that is to say we know there are some things we do not know. But there are also unknown unknowns – the ones we don't know we don't know."

In fact risk management is not difficult. It simply offers a structured way to think about risk, providing a framework to channel how we deal with risk intuitively. At its foundation, risk management involves asking and answering a few simple questions:

- What are we trying to achieve and how much risk can we take? (setting objectives and risk thresholds).
- What risks might affect us, either to help or hinder? (risk identification).
- Which of these are most important? (qualitative risk assessment).
- How could these affect our overall outcome? (quantitative risk analysis).
- What shall we do about it? (risk response development and implementation).
- Who needs to know about this? (risk reporting).
- Having taken action, how did our responses change things and where are we now? (risk review).
- What have we learned? (lessons-learned review).

These questions represent the simplest expression of an intuitive risk management process. They can easily be expanded into a more detailed process that represents a natural and logical approach for managing risk in a business or project, indicating the extent to which risk management is simply structured common sense. We'll return to this in Chapter 3.

There is a second sense in which some people view risk management as "hard." This is in contrast to other disciplines that are regarded as "soft" because they are more concerned with people than with techniques. Risk management involves the use of brainstorming, checklists, Risk Registers, probability-impact matrices, Monte Carlo simulation, decision trees etc.

All these are hard analytical techniques that require discipline, rigour and structure, based on data and numbers. Other management skills such as team forming, motivation, leadership, conflict resolution, communication and so on are "soft skills" based not on numbers but on the need to understand how people tick – a fascinating subject we will look into in the People chapter of this book (Chapter 4).

But this is also true of risk management. Machines, computers or robots do not manage risk: people do. Every step of the risk process involves people: we set objectives and risk thresholds, identify and assess risks, propose and implement responses etc. Yet each individual has a distinct personality, history, set of motivations and needs, relationships etc. These characteristics influence how people react to risk, both on their own and when in groups, leading them to adopt risk attitudes that vary between situations and with time.

Without taking proper account of the people aspects of managing risk, the risk process will be subject to unseen influences, leading to unreliable results and actions. Conversely, when attitudes and behaviours are fully understood and managed, then the risk process will work as it should. Effective management of risk in projects and the wider business requires both people and process, acting together to allow risk to be managed intelligently and appropriately.

Risk management isn't hard, it's easy, because it embodies an intuitive process for dealing with uncertainty that matters, and most people will find it natural. And risk management isn't hard, it's soft as well, because it requires both the use of structured techniques as well as the ability to understand and manage people. If we persist in the view that risk management is hard it will encourage people not to do it. But if we recognise that managing risk is basically not difficult and that it needs to take proper account of people, it will be much more effective in helping us to deliver our goals.

WHAT ABOUT LUCK?

Yes, luck has a part to play in business, as well as risk management. We often wish each other "Good luck" as we embark on a new enterprise, especially if it involves something new or untried. But is it appropriate for risk practitioners to mention luck? Surely that's rather unprofessional, and we should be aiming to manage risk rather than hoping to be lucky. Well yes and no.

Let's start with a definition: Luck is "an unknown and unpredictable phenomenon that causes an event to result one way rather than another." It comes in two varieties: good luck, when something pleasant happens unexpectedly; and bad luck, when we get a nasty surprise and an unwelcome thing happens. In this way, luck is like risk – an uncertain future event that, if it happens, matters. Remember that risk also has two varieties: threats and opportunities. So wishing someone "Good luck" is the same as hoping that some unplanned opportunities happen for them.

Of course, luck happens to everyone, including both bad luck and good luck (in the same way that risk affects us all). The important thing is what you do with it. There are two areas to consider if we are to avoid being mere victims of whatever luck happens to us.

First, we should be ready for luck, whether good or bad. If you have an unwelcome surprise at work, what will you do? Will you react out of panic, or be paralysed into doing nothing? Or will you respond with a pre-prepared contingency plan, perhaps including elements of crisis management, disaster recovery or business continuity if necessary?

Luck happens to everyone, including both bad luck and good luck. The important thing is what you do with it.

And what happens if you have some good luck? Will you be so surprised that you do nothing and waste it, or will you have a contingency plan to take advantage of the unexpected benefit? As Louis Pasteur said, **"Chance only favours the prepared mind."** Or in the words of Roman philosopher Seneca, **"Luck is what happens when preparation meets opportunity."**

Second, we don't have to just wait to see what luck materialises. We can make our own luck. Golfer Gary Player noticed that, **"The harder I practice, the luckier I get."** Archbishop William Temple had a similar experience saying, **"When I pray, coincidences happen, and when I don't, they don't."** If we discover and tackle the roots of bad luck, we can reduce its frequency and severity. In the same way, finding and reinforcing the causes of good luck can lead to more nice surprises. The important thing is not how lucky you are, it's what you do with the luck you get. So as well as urging you to manage risk effectively, l wish you "Good luck" – and the wisdom to know how to handle it.

> " Luck is what happens when
> preparation meets opportunity."
> Seneca

PROVE IT! THE VALUE OF MANAGING RISK

It would be great if we could simply calculate Return On Investment (ROI) for risk management, with unambiguous metrics for determining whether a risk management process is effective, clearly showing a link between risk management and improved bottom-line outcomes.

If only we could prove in advance the value of doing good risk management, for example to convince management or a client that risk assessment should be undertaken in order to develop appropriate response strategies. Guidelines on how to demonstrate success in risk management would be really useful, identifying the critical success factors? Can we quantify the beneficial impact of risk management through some type of cost-benefit analysis and combine that with an estimate of how much risk management costs in order to calculate an ROI?

Unfortunately it's difficult to design an academic research project to answer these questions directly. This leaves an important and vexing question for risk practitioners – how do we prove we're adding value?! If academic research can't help us, is there any other practical way of demonstrating that risk management is working?

We will discuss costs and benefits in the next two sections. In the meantime, part of the problem is the perception that risk management can seem to be a waste of time and money. If risk was successfully managed, then nothing would happen, at least there would be no unpleasant surprises, and everything would go according to plan. But how do we know that the lack of problems is due to successful risk management? Perhaps we were just lucky? Or perhaps there were no real risks anyway? So maybe we should stop wasting our efforts trying to manage things that may not exist, or that may never happen even if they do exist, and instead concentrate on the real tasks in hand. Real work is more important than theoretical risks, right?

Here are three practical suggestions to persuade the sceptics that risk management is worth doing.

1   Firstly, if risk management were only about threats, successful risk management would indeed mean that "nothing happens". In line with Popper's Falsifiability Principle, we know it's impossible to prove a negative, even though absence of evidence is not evidence of absence. So we couldn't say for certain that investing in risk management was positively correlated with lack of problems.

    However now we have a new view of risk that includes opportunities as well as threats. Now successful risk management should address threats and result in avoiding problems as before, but it should also create additional value through maximising and exploiting opportunities. And of course this can be measured.

> If we track performance, we should be able to see if there is any link between our ability to manage risk and our success rate.

2 Secondly, it's true that we cannot run the same project twice or make an identical decision a second time, so we have no control for proving risk management effectiveness, at least in projects. We can't do it once with risk management and once without, and see what difference the risk process makes to the outcome.

But we can learn from our experience over time. If we track performance over a number of years, measuring how good our decision-making is or how often we deliver on time, within budget, with full scope etc, we should be able to see if there is any link between our ability to manage risk and our success rate. Perhaps we could demonstrate that as risk management maturity and competence increases, so does success.

3 Thirdly, the value of risk management will be obvious if we emphasise the close link between risk and objectives. Risk is defined as "any uncertain event or condition that, if it occurs, will have a positive or negative effect on achievement of objectives." The point of the risk process is to minimise threats and maximise opportunities, so that we can optimise achievement of objectives. This makes the relationship between managing risk and business success clear. If we fail to manage risk effectively, then unmanaged threats will turn into problems that result in delays, additional cost, destroyed value etc. Ineffective risk management will also lead to missed opportunities, denying us the benefits that we could have gained if we'd been able to capture some of those opportunities. We need to understand that there are distinct bottom-line benefits. We do risk management because it delivers value and helps us to succeed, not because we have to.

Perhaps it is better that we don't rely on the academics to tell us whether risk management works or not. Managing risk is essentially a practical task, done on the ground by hard-pressed teams who need to see results. We need to do it properly, and see what happens. We should expect to be hit by fewer problems as we manage threats successfully, but also to find ways of saving time and money as we capture opportunities. We should see our success rate improving with time in line with our ability to manage risk effectively. And we should demonstrably increase our ability to achieve objectives as a direct result of managing those risks that could affect them. Otherwise why would we bother?

WHAT'S THE COST?

$$\text{ROI} = \frac{\text{RETURN (benefit)}}{\text{INVESTMENT (cost)}}$$

The previous section asked an important and valid question: "What is the Return On Investment (ROI)?" and many organisations considering whether to invest in risk management would like an answer. ROI has two components: the amount invested (cost), and the return achieved (benefit). Calculating ROI is therefore essentially a cost-benefit analysis. While the benefits from effectively managing risk are clear and many (and we'll deal with those next), the cost question is not simple. Risk management is not free; it must be paid for somehow, but is it worth it? There is no "zero-cost option" for risk management, and the costs to be paid fall into three categories: one-off, ongoing, and operational.

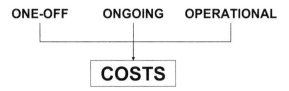

First are the **one-off entry costs**, paid once by an organisation to establish its initial risk management capability. The primary cost here is for the "Three Ts": techniques, tools and training. Any organisation wishing to manage risk has to invest in the necessary infrastructure to support the risk process. Techniques and procedures must be developed and rolled out. Tools to support the process must be bought or developed. And staff must be trained to use the techniques and tools effectively. If the entry cost is not paid, risk management remains merely a good intention, with no capability to deliver.

> There is no "zero-cost option"
> for risk management

The second type are **ongoing maintenance costs**, to preserve an effective organisational risk management capability. It is important to keep the risk process fresh and up to date. Without ongoing development of the risk process, there is a danger of losing effectiveness. Risk management is a developing discipline, and new techniques and tools emerge regularly. Even the conceptual basis continues to grow as new ideas become accepted into the mainstream. And new staff joining the organisation may lack the necessary competence or understanding. Effective risk management requires refresher training to maintain and develop staff skills, as well as revitalising the process to incorporate recent developments. On average an organisation should aim to refresh its risk process every 2–3 years to stay up to date.

Thirdly there are the **operational costs** associated with managing risk in business. Many aspects of the risk challenge are unique, and managing this challenge incurs costs both for assessing risk and for addressing risk.

- **Assessing risk**
  These are the costs of implementing the risk process, including spending time and resources in risk identification workshops or interviews, performing risk assessments and analyses, attending risk reviews, producing and maintaining the Risk Register, writing risk reports etc.

- **Addressing risk**
  This covers the cost of executing risk response plans, those actions which were not originally planned, but which are now deemed necessary in order to deal appropriately with identified risks. Proactive actions are needed to address both threats and opportunities, and the costs of these actions fall under two headings: "Spend to save" (avoid or reduce threats) and "Spend to gain" (exploit or enhance opportunities). Contingency and fallback plans must also be put in place in case risks occur. These costs would not have been incurred if risks had not been identified, but they are necessary to optimise the chances of achieving objectives.

If an organisation is serious about managing its risk, it must be prepared to pay all of these types of costs. This is particularly true of projects, which tend to have fixed budgets. Risk management will never be effective if it is seen as an optional zero-cost extra. The cost of assessing risk must be included in the overall project management budget, and there must be adequate contingency in the project budget to cover the costs of addressing risks.

In addition to these "hard costs" which can be measured in cash or effort, there are also the "soft costs" of developing and maintaining a risk-aware culture. These include a top-down commitment to implementing risk management across the organisation, a committed and proactive risk-aware attitude that recognises risk and is determined to address it, and a degree of organisational courage required to operate confidently in an uncertain environment in order to gain the rewards available from embracing risk. While these soft costs may be hard to quantify, they form an essential component of the investment required if an organisation is to gain the full benefit from its risk management process.

> Not paying the cost to implement risk management exposes an organisation to a hidden cost – the impact of unmanaged risk.

Of course there is a cost-benefit relationship from investing in risk management. Risk management delivers a wide range of benefits to the organisation and to its projects, clients and staff. Although it may be hard to measure the Return On Investment for risk management, it is certain that no benefits will be realised unless the organisation is prepared to pay these costs.

Indeed, not paying the cost to implement risk management exposes an organisation to a hidden cost – the impact of unmanaged risk. This includes avoidable threats which turn into problems, missed opportunities which could have delivered extra value, more failed projects delivering reduced business benefits, dissatisfied clients and damaged reputations, demotivated staff with reduced productivity, and so on.

Is risk management worth it? The answer is a definite yes – if we pay the cost we will reap the benefits.

WHY BOTHER? THE BENEFITS

Having counted the cost of risk management, it is time to turn to the second component of the cost-benefit analysis, namely benefits. What does risk management offer in return for investment from the organisation? There are many benefits arising from a proactive and structured approach to managing risk. These are found at different levels in the business, starting with projects, but also including managers, teams, and the wider organisation.

A business with an effective risk process will experience fewer surprises as it deploys the forward-looking radar of risk management. Predictability is valued by many businesses, and the ability to look ahead and spot potential problems and benefits is key to success. Being able to do something about those potential problems and benefits is even better, of course! Every business would benefit from minimising threats to achievement of its objectives, as well as maximising opportunities to work faster, smarter and cheaper.

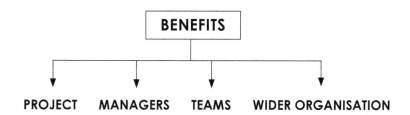

At **project level**, effective risk management leads to more successful projects, delivered on time, within budget and with full scope. Waste and rework are minimised, both as a result of realistic initial plans and because of improved flexibility and resilience to change. Risk assessment also improves the ability to determine the impact on risk exposure of proposed or imposed changes. Where risk remains (as it surely will), an appropriate level of risk contingency can be allocated, and the people best able to manage residual risk can be identified.

> A business with an effective risk process will experience fewer surprises as it deploys the forward-looking radar of risk management.

The benefits of managing risk are found across the business. The **manager** in charge of a project group or department where risks are managed proactively and effectively will reap a range of personal rewards. These include an enhanced personal and professional reputation, becoming known as a person who can deal with risk and deliver successful results. This is likely to lead to career enhancement, perhaps in the form of promotion or allocation to more challenging and high-profile assignments. A higher professional standing might also create new opportunities in the wider management community, improving openings for networking and development.

On a personal note, becoming more risk-aware will lead to less fire-fighting and fewer crises, reducing stress levels both for the manager and the team. The manager will also be able to focus the team on key issues, addressing the worst threats and the best opportunities. Team members and other resources can be concentrated in the highest-risk areas, maximising effectiveness. Where additional resources are required, an effective risk process can support the manager's call for assistance, providing senior management with a justified case for intervention.

Team members will find work more fulfilling and more fun, as they are able to concentrate on what matters. Knowing that unplanned changes will be kept to a minimum and that the business is well controlled will improve motivation and lead to higher productivity. The team will also appreciate the platform provided by the risk process where they can express their concerns about the things that might affect success. Being able to do this in a safe environment without personal blame is an important benefit for team members. The process also acts as a framework for them to make a significant contribution to success, as they identify threats and opportunities, propose responses, and implement actions to change risk exposure. Being able to affect risk exposure directly will lead to higher morale and a sense of ownership among team members.

Finally there are clear benefits to the **wider organisation** from having risk managed effectively. These include more satisfied clients whose requirements are delivered successfully. This enhances the organisation's reputation and should lead to more work and better work. In fact effective risk management creates competitive advantage, both through improved delivery and also through the ability to produce better bids and proposals. The organisation improves its risk-awareness and learns how to take the right level of risk into the business.

A clear understanding of organisational risk appetite allows a risk-balanced portfolio to be built and managed, avoiding bad projects or investments that breach the risk threshold. As the organisation learns from experience about the risk inherent in its business, it should be able to modify standard operating procedures to reduce the cost base and maximise margin or profit. And finally people will want to work for an organisation where risk is managed effectively. This will allow the business to recruit and retain the best staff at all levels.

So there are multiple benefits available from managing risk. Many of the benefits outlined here can be measured, although there are certainly a significant number of intangible benefits (which are not less important of course). Combining these benefits with an assessment of the costs of managing risk allows us to estimate the Return On Investment (ROI) for risk management. Although managing risk is not free, the wide range of benefits available offers clear support for the assertion: **"Risk management is good for you!"**

DOES RISK MANAGEMENT CRUSH INNOVATION?

"Risk management is the antithesis of innovation." Wrong!

Risk management is most effective when it considers both threats and opportunities. Surely achieving this goal requires a great deal of innovation in the risk process?

> "If you always do what you always did, you'll always get what you've always got!"

The first area where creativity is essential is in risk identification. This requires thinking the unthinkable, not being constrained by "the Plan", but considering other options and alternatives. It asks questions such as "What if… Why not… If only… How about…?" Potential problems (threats) and unexpected benefits (opportunities) can be identified using a range of creative techniques, including brainstorming, assumptions-busting, root-cause analysis, visualisation, scenario analysis, or futures thinking. Indeed it is probably not possible to identify risks without being innovative and thinking new thoughts.

But a second part of the risk process also requires fresh thinking, namely development of effective risk responses. Einstein reputedly said, **"It is not possible to solve a problem using the same thinking that created it."** Just identifying risks is not enough, and if appropriate action is not taken then risk exposure will remain unchanged. However deciding what is "appropriate" for each risk demands a degree of innovation, being prepared to consider and implement actions that were previously not thought necessary.

Einstein also defined insanity as, **"Doing the same thing over and over again and expecting different results"**, which might be rephrased as, **"If you always do what you always did, you'll always get what you've always got!"** As the Chinese proverb says, **"If we don't change direction we're likely to end up where we're headed."**

However the link between innovation and risk management is not just in the process. In fact innovation is at the heart of the reason for doing risk management at all. If we didn't innovate there would be no risk. Doing the same old thing with which we're fully familiar, repeating tasks we've done many times before, knowing exactly how the future will turn out – there is no risk associated with this type of activity, except perhaps the risk of dying from terminal boredom.

It is only when we step outside our comfort zone into an unfamiliar place that we expose ourselves to risk. And this is the realm of projects and business, where we try to do something unique in a way that creates benefits and value for stakeholders. It is in the very nature of projects and business to take risks, recognising that risk is related to reward. Playing it safe will never bring big returns – these are reserved for the organisations and individuals who are prepared to step outside the ordinary, change the rules of the game, and dare to be different.

This type of risk-taking demands a structured approach to managing risk – which is why risk management is inextricably linked to innovation. The companies, projects and individuals that know they need to take risk in order to innovate and be creative also recognise that they must proceed with an appropriate degree of caution. The trick is to balance the amount of attention given to risk management with the need to innovate.

Anyone who believes that "Risk management is the antithesis of innovation" is probably reacting to an outdated caricature of risk management. If the aim of risk management is perceived as preventing variation from plan at all costs, desperately clinging to the original approach and refusing all change, then it is true that creativity and innovation will be stifled. But modern risk management is very different. It actively embraces and welcomes change, recognising that some risks present an opportunity to improve on the original plan by working "smarter, faster, cheaper" – there is upside as well as downside.

"Uncreative risk management" is an oxymoron that cannot exist, and risk management without innovation merely rehearses and records the inevitable. To be effective the risk process must embody innovative and creative thinking in both risk identification and response development, proactively seeking potentially significant uncertainties and addressing them appropriately. It must also support and encourage innovation in projects and businesses, allowing them to move forward and take appropriate risks safely. Anything less does not deserve to be called risk management.

WHAT ABOUT MATURITY?

Today's society often debates the value of age. The demographic time bomb can't be defused, and coping with our increasingly aging population will demand changes in many aspects of society. In what some call "yoof culcha", experience is not valued, older people are seen as irrelevant and unproductive, and the ideal human state is to be young, strong and beautiful. This thinking has even permeated the business world, where traditional ways of working are regarded as outdated, and everything needs to be the latest version. The rise of change management as a driving discipline is perhaps a symptom of this approach.

In parallel with these developments, we have seen a contrasting focus on maturity in many parts of corporate life. The Irish poet John Finlay defined maturity as "the capacity to endure uncertainty", and as we face increasing uncertainty all around us, more and more organisations aspire to maturity in a range of areas of competence, including risk management.

There has been a rapid growth in so-called "maturity models" which claim to measure degrees of capability in various disciplines, aiming to help organisations become "more mature". The better risk management maturity models take a broad view across the many factors required for competence in managing risk, for example addressing the risk culture of an organisation, as well as its risk processes, its risk infrastructure, and the risk knowledge and skills of its people.

"Maturity is the capacity to endure uncertainty"
John Finlay

Clearly people see maturity as desirable, a goal to which every organisation should aspire. But is it always a good thing? Or is it possible to be too mature? The word "mature" is used in at least two ways. One meaning is about being fully developed, ripe, at the peak of perfection, having reached the maximum level of development. But the word is also used to mean no longer young, with implications of being old and past it. Brigitte Bardot recognised this dual meaning when she reportedly said, "I have not grown old, I have ripened."

So what is "risk management maturity"? Does it mean that the approach to risk management in a particular organisation has developed as far as it can, no further improvement is possible, and everything is as good as it's going to get? Or does it imply a degree of inflexibility, being set in one's ways, in a rut, and doing things because "we've always done it that way"? Neither of these seems to be an attractive option or a worthwhile goal.

Perhaps it is possible to be "too mature"? Some older people seem to think they are so mature that they never need or expect to learn anything new, while others recognise the falsehood in the statement that, "You can't teach an old dog new tricks." The same is true of organisations, with some believing that they are at the top of their game and just need to keep doing what they're doing, perhaps with incremental improvements, and others constantly seeking to innovate and reinvent themselves to meet the challenges and opportunities of the moment – the so-called "Madonna approach". Maybe a perception of "being mature" might discourage people or organisations from wanting change, if they don't see the need. In that sense, maturity could be a dangerous thing.

So what is the answer? One answer might be to proactively reduce one's level of maturity, to deliberately "de-mature". This might involve challenging the accepted way of doing things, seeking to cut out aspects of risk management process and practice that have grown up over time but which are no longer necessary. We can learn from the "lean" and "agile" movements here, identifying and removing redundancy and waste, and seeking to maximise efficiency while retaining full effectiveness. "Lean risk management" may be the way of the future.

An alternative answer we can implement more immediately is to ensure that our approach to risk management is constantly refreshed and renewed. This might involve adopting new techniques, keeping up to date with the latest thinking and developments, learning from leading practitioners in our own and other industries, offering refresher skills training to our staff etc.

We all need to beware of complacency, especially in risk management. In our ever-changing world, what worked yesterday may not be good enough for today or tomorrow. When considering whether to ripen like Bardot or adapt like Madonna, we should remember that age is no guarantee of maturity!

PROBLEMS WITH RISK APPETITE

People and their attitude to risk is a central theme to this book. According to recent government statistics, three-quarters of Britons are overweight, more than one-fifth are obese, and over a quarter claim to be on a diet at any one time. Weight is clearly a national obsession, on a par with the weather. And obesity is not just a physical problem in Britain today. The nation is suffering from an epidemic of risk-obesity, resulting from uncontrolled risk appetite in recent years. This has affected credit-hungry individuals and organisations as much as financial institutions, as many of us have embarked on a risk binge characterised by greed, naivety and lack of concern for the future implications. Now we have seen the danger signs as the amount of risk taken on board has reached staggering proportions, and we all know something must be done.

The physical world offers a range of metaphors to illustrate how we might respond to the realisation that we have become risk-obese. These offer warnings and helpful models for both individuals and organisations that feel they have taken on too much risk and need to do something about it. It is useful to draw on medical metaphors, but I must emphasise I do not intend to deny the reality of the genuine medical conditions mentioned, or to belittle or undermine the challenges faced by those who suffer from them.

One condition suffered by some individuals and organisations that become aware of overexposure to risk might be described as risk-anorexia. This is characterised by an extreme rejection of risk from any source, driven by a distorted image of the current situation as being too risky. The result is risk-starvation, refusing to be exposed to any downside risk in case it gets out of control. This obsession can also mean refusing to try new situations where there might be upside risk. While risk exposure will certainly reduce under these circumstances, overall health can be endangered and lasting damage might be done.

> The nation is suffering from an epidemic of risk-obesity, resulting from uncontrolled risk appetite in recent years.

A similar problem might be called risk-bulimia, resulting in a repeated cycle of taking on too much risk followed by a forced risk reduction. The binge-purge sequence can be driven by a compulsion to take a lot of risk which then triggers feelings of guilt or fear of being overexposed, leading to a strong desire to get rid of risk at any cost.

Both of these conditions are clearly unhealthy, but they can exert a strong influence over behaviour that can be hard to break. Fortunately there is another response to being risk-obese that does not bring the same problems. The best answer to being in a situation where risk exposure is too high is to follow a balanced risk-diet, aiming to reduce overall risk exposure in a steady and controlled manner until the right level is reached.

The detail of the risk-diet will be different for each individual or organisation, and the degree of risk exposure will need careful monitoring to ensure that it remains within acceptable bounds.

A specific level of acceptable risk threshold should be set so that progress towards the goal can be measured, and so that we will know when to stop reducing. Just as each individual has a different ideal weight, so the appropriate target level of risk exposure will vary between individuals and organisations. And instant results are not to be expected; moving from risk-obesity to a proper degree of risk will take time.

General health must be also maintained during the dieting period, giving attention to the usual processes of life such as exercise, work, rest and relationships. Similarly organisations seeking to reduce their risk exposure should not ignore other aspects of the business in the drive to shed risk, but must continue to manage client relationships, staff morale, marketing and communication etc.

Finally when the target is reached, new risk habits must be established. We need to be aware of our risk appetite and manage it proactively on a daily basis. Do I feel hungry to take on more risk? Is that appropriate now, or should I resist the risk-seeking urge? Am I getting a balanced diet, including the right range of nutrients that will promote healthy growth? Or is there an area where taking on more risk or a different type of risk would bring useful rewards? Does my output match my intake, with sufficient activity to take advantage of the risk I have taken on board?

One last metaphor might be useful in this context. Anyone who has ever dieted will know that it is very common to gain weight when you stop dieting. The "diet rebound effect" occurs because lower calorie consumption during the diet results in a slowing of the body's metabolism. When we return to normal eating habits after the diet ends, the metabolic rate remains low and extra calories are stored as fat, leading to increased weight.

As society, individuals and organisations seek to reduce their risk exposure in the coming months and years, the general rate at which we absorb risk may settle to a lower level than it has been before. When we return to some semblance of economic normality, we will need to be careful not to become risk-overweight again due to the risk-rebound effect. Instead we need to find a new normal that fits our new circumstances, setting appropriate risk thresholds and controlling our risk appetite to ensure that we maintain good health and continued growth.

HOW IS IT FOR YOU?

How do you view risk management? How important is it – and how effective?

Recent Risk Doctor research investigated how organisations perceive the value of risk management. The survey addressed a number of different aspects, but two questions were particularly interesting. The first question asked, "How important is risk management to your success?" with possible answers chosen from extremely important, very important, important, somewhat important, not important. The second question asked, "How effective is risk management in your organisation?", with answers ranging from extremely effective, very effective, effective, somewhat effective, or ineffective. Of course the raw data was interesting in itself, but the correlation between answers to these two questions was fascinating.

If the answers to each question are simplified into two options (positive or negative), there are four possible combinations, shown in the illustration together with how many organisations chose each one:

1 **Risk management is important and effective.**
2 **Risk management is important but not effective.**
3 **Risk management is not important and not effective.**
4 **Risk management is not important but it is (somehow) effective.**

Perhaps the fourth combination is not really feasible, since it would be unusual for risk management to be effective if the organisation does not consider it to be important. In fact only 1% of people responding to the research questionnaire believed themselves to be in this situation. Indeed if it is viewed as unimportant it might not be done at all. But the other three combinations represent different levels of risk management maturity, and organisations in each of these three groups might be expected to act in very different ways.

Where risk management is seen as important and it is also effectively delivering the promised benefits (Combination 1), those organisations can be champions for risk management, demonstrating how it can work, and persuading others to follow their lead. These risk-mature organisations can blow the trumpet to allow others to learn from their good experience. Encouragingly, over 40% of respondents in the research project reported being in this position.

If an organisation believes that risk management is important but is not finding it to be effective in practice (Combination 2), which was the position reported by about 40% of respondents, they should consider launching an improvement initiative to benchmark and develop their risk management capability. Tackling the Critical Success Factors (CSFs) for effective risk management will lead to enhanced capability and maturity, allowing the organisation to reap the expected benefits. Key CSFs include a risk-aware culture, efficient processes, experienced and skilled staff, and consistent application.

It is not surprising that risk management is ineffective in organisations that believe that it is unimportant (Combination 3), as it is not possible to manage risk effectively without some degree of commitment and buy-in. Only 17% of respondents admitted to this, perhaps recognising that it was not a particularly good place to be. These risk-immature organisations can be persuaded and educated about the benefits of risk management to the business – a task best performed by convinced insiders who can show how proactive management of risk could be applied to meet the specific challenges of the organisation.

Risk management offers genuine and significant benefits to organisations, their projects and their stakeholders, but these will never be achieved without recognition of the importance of managing risk at all levels in the business, matched with operational effectiveness in executing risk management in practice.

> Risk management is ineffective in organisations that believe that it is unimportant.

Have you worked out where you stand? Read on. Our next chapter covers the concepts of risk management, then we'll look at its practical application.

2

Risk Concepts

UNIVERSAL LAWS OF RISK MANAGEMENT

The term "risk management" covers many different types of risk, including strategic risk, financial risk, reputational risk, operational risk, project risk, environmental risk, legal risk, contract risk, or technical risk, as well as corporate governance, business continuity and disaster recovery. While each of these areas has its own special language, processes and techniques, there are some principles that apply to them all. These might be called "universal laws of risk management".

> I   RISK IS UNCERTAIN
>
> II   RISK MATTERS
>
> III   USE RISK PROCESS
>
> IV   PEOPLE MANAGE RISK

The first law of risk management: Risk is uncertain

A risk is something in the future that might or might not occur. This is vital to a proper understanding of risk and its management. Risks do not yet exist, indeed they may never exist at all. They are potential future events or sets of circumstances or conditions. This makes them quite different from things which have happened in the past or which currently exist in the present. Past and present events can be analysed and measured, but future events can only be imagined or estimated. A risk that may or may not come to pass in the future cannot be experienced directly unless or until it happens. This makes risks different from issues, problems or constraints. In every type of risk management, risk is in the future, which is inherently uncertain.

The second law of risk management: Risk matters

If they occur, risks will have consequences that make a difference in some way. It is not possible to have an inconsequential risk, by definition. While various types of risk management focus on different sorts of consequence, all agree that a risk must affect something. This is because risks are inextricably linked to objectives. Wherever some field of human endeavour is attempting to achieve something, it is possible to identify uncertainties that might affect the chances of success. Whether the objectives are to achieve good corporate governance, successful projects or business continuity, risk management aims to identify possible future events that could influence those objectives, and to enable them to be understood and managed effectively.

The third law of risk management: Managing risk is a process

They may have different steps, but all approaches to risk management provide a framework that is designed to maximise both efficiency and effectiveness. Although the details of risk processes are different, every type of risk management has two important parts: analysis and action. Before risk can be properly managed, it must first be identified, described, understood and assessed. Analysis is a necessary first step but it is not sufficient – it must be followed by action. The ultimate aim is to manage risk, not simply to identify it.

The fourth of risk management: Risk is managed by people

The human aspects of risk management are vital to its success and effectiveness. People implement processes, though we may use machines to automate calculations, to record results, or to generate reports. People set risk thresholds, identify risks, assess the degree of uncertainty and extent of possible impact, propose appropriate responses and implement agreed actions. These require judgements, estimates and decisions to be made in the presence of uncertainty. These judgements are subject to a range of influences, both explicit and hidden, which can significantly affect the outcome. Risk management at every level is exposed to sources of bias arising from overt and covert influences acting on individuals and groups who are trying to make risk-based decisions with imperfect or incomplete information.

Whatever type of risk we face, we have to follow these universal laws of risk management. To manage risk effectively we need to deal with **uncertainty** that **matters**, follow a **structured process**, and take account of the **people aspects**.

WHAT EXACTLY IS A RISK? (AND WHAT ISN'T)

One of the most common failings in the risk management process is for the risk identification step to identify things that are not risks. Clearly if this early stage of the risk process fails, subsequent steps will be doomed and risk management cannot be effective. It is therefore essential to ensure that risk identification identifies risks. There are two key requirements for effective risk identification. The first is a clear understanding of what is meant by the term "risk". The second is to be able to distinguish risks from non-risks, particularly from their causes and effects.

Many people when they try to identify risks get confused between risk and uncertainty. Risk is not the same as uncertainty, so how are the two related? The key is to realise that risk can only be defined in relation to objectives. The simplest definition of risk is "uncertainty that matters", and it matters because it can affect one or more objectives. Risk cannot exist in a vacuum, and we need to define what is "at risk", i.e. what objectives would be affected if the risk occurred.

A more complete definition of risk would therefore be "an uncertainty that if it occurs could affect one or more objectives". This recognises the fact that there are other uncertainties that are irrelevant in terms of objectives, and these should be excluded from the risk process. For example if we are conducting an IT project in India, the uncertainty

about whether it might be raining tomorrow in London is irrelevant –
who cares? But if our project involves redeveloping the Queen's gardens
at Buckingham Palace, the possibility of rain in London is not just an
uncertainty – it matters. In one case the rain is merely an irrelevant
uncertainty, but in the other it is a risk.

Linking risk with objectives makes it clear that every facet of life
is risky. Everything we do aims to achieve objectives of some sort,
including personal objectives (for example, to be happy and healthy),
project objectives (including delivering on time and within budget),
and corporate business objectives (such as to increase profit and market
share). Wherever objectives are defined, there will be risks to their
successful achievement.

The link also helps us to identify risks at different levels, based on
the hierarchy of objectives that exists in an organisation. For example
strategic risks are uncertainties that could affect strategic objectives,
programme risks might affect programme objectives, tactical risks would
affect tactical objectives, and so on. We can also use it to find different
specialised types of risk by focusing on the objective affected, including
reputation risks, environmental, health & safety or technical risks, each
of which affects a different type of objective.

> Linking risks with objectives will ensure
> that risk identification focuses on
> uncertainties that matter, rather than
> irrelevant uncertainties.

One other question arises from the concept of risk as "uncertainty that could affect objectives": what sort of effect might occur? In addition to those uncertainties which if they occur would make it more difficult to achieve objectives (also known as threats), there are also uncertain events which if they occur would help us achieve our objectives (i.e. opportunities). When identifying risks, we need to look for uncertainties with upside as well as those with downside.

Effective risk management requires identification of real risks, which are "uncertainties which if they occur will have a positive or negative effect on one or more objectives". Linking risks with objectives will ensure that the risk identification process focuses on those uncertainties that matter, rather than being distracted and diverted by irrelevant uncertainties.

Another common challenge in risk identification is to avoid confusion between causes of risk, genuine risks, and the effects of risks. The Project Management Institute's *Guide to the Project Management Body of Knowledge* (PMBoK®) says that, "A risk may have one or more causes and, if it occurs, one or more impacts". In the most simple case, one cause leads to a single risk that in turn could have just one effect (as illustrated below), though of course reality is considerably more complex.

CAUSE — Definite fact about situation or its environment

RISK — Uncertainty that would matter if it occurs

EFFECT — Contingent effect of risk on objective(s)

How do these three differ?

- **Causes** are definite events or sets of circumstances which exist in the business, the project or the environment, and which give rise to uncertainty. Examples include the requirement to implement a project in a developing country, the need to use an unproven new technology, the lack of skilled personnel, or the fact that the organisation has never launched a similar product before. Causes themselves are not uncertain since they are facts or requirements, so they are not the main focus of the risk management process.

- **Risks** are uncertainties, which, if they occur, would affect achievement of the objectives either negatively (threats) or positively (opportunities). Examples include the possibility that planned productivity targets might not be met, interest or exchange rates might fluctuate, the chance that client expectations may be misunderstood, or whether a contractor might deliver earlier than planned. These uncertainties should be managed proactively through the risk management process.

- **Effects** are unplanned variations from objectives, either positive or negative, which would arise as a result of risks occurring. Examples include being early for a milestone, exceeding the authorised budget, or failing to meet contractually agreed performance targets. Effects are contingent events, unplanned potential future variations that will not occur unless risks happen. As effects do not yet exist, and indeed they may never exist, they cannot be managed proactively through the risk management process.

Including causes or effects in the list of identified risks obscures genuine risks, which may not receive the appropriate degree of attention they deserve. So how can we clearly separate risks from their causes and effects? One way is to use risk metalanguage (a formal description with required elements) to provide a three-part structured "risk statement", as follows: "As a result of <one or more definite causes>, <uncertain event> may occur, which would lead to <one or more effects on objective(s)>."

Examples include the following:

- "As a result of using novel hardware (a definite requirement), unexpected system integration errors may occur (an uncertain risk), which would lead to overspend on the project (an effect on the budget objective)."

- "Because our organisation has never done a project like this before (fact = cause), we might misunderstand the customer's requirement (uncertainty = risk), and our solution would not meet the performance criteria (contingent possibility = effect on objective)."

- "We have to outsource production (cause); we may be able to learn new practices from our selected partner (risk), leading to increased productivity and profitability (effect)."

The use of risk metalanguage should ensure that risk identification actually identifies risks, distinct from causes or effects. Without this discipline, risk identification can produce a mixed list containing risks and non-risks, leading to confusion and distraction later in the risk process. We must therefore concentrate our risk management process on addressing those uncertainties that can affect our business.

WHY RISK INCLUDES OPPORTUNITY

We have seen how "risk" is now widely accepted to encompass opportunity as well as threat. Yet some people are still unsure about using the risk process to identify and capture opportunities, although it makes sense for three reasons:

> Including opportunity within the definition of risk is not a theoretical or academic exercise driven by a misplaced desire for symmetry.

1 Conceptual

Risk can be viewed as a source of potential variability in performance, since if risks were to occur they would affect our ability to achieve our goals. Variability is a two-sided construct, since most variables can go both up and down. For example if there is uncertainty about the productivity rate of a team, it could be higher than planned or lower. Weather might be better or worse than expected. System integration might find more or fewer bugs than usual. This double-sided nature of variability is captured in definitions of risk that include both upside and downside consequences.

More generally, risk has been described as "uncertainty that matters", i.e. a possible future event that would be significant if it occurred. This clearly includes threats, which might occur and which would cause problems if they did. But an opportunity is also uncertain since it is a possible future event, and it matters because it would be helpful if it occurred. So both threats and opportunities are covered by the same description of risk as "uncertainty that matters".

2 Practical

Threats and opportunities are important, and they both need to be managed. Dealing with them together in an integrated risk process brings synergies and efficiencies. Most organisations have a process for dealing with downside risks, and simply extending this process to include upside risks will deliver additional benefits for little extra cost or effort.

Opportunities can be found by using standard risk identification techniques, for example workshops, assumptions testing, SWOT (Strengths, Weaknesses, Opportunities and Threats) analysis or root-cause analysis. They can be prioritised in the same way as threats, by assessing probability and impact, or other relevant attributes. Opportunity response strategies mirror those used for threats. Reporting formats such as Risk Registers can be simply adapted to include both opportunities and threats. It is easy to implement a combined risk process to manage both threats and opportunities alongside each other.

3 Beneficial

A structured approach to identifying and capturing opportunities is good for business and for projects. It gives people a structured framework to find and implement ways of working "faster, smarter, cheaper". This supports innovation and creativity, and is highly motivating for teams who want to maximise the value they deliver. A broader inclusive risk process means that opportunities will be sought proactively, and some will be identified and captured which might otherwise have been missed.

This will deliver more value than relying on luck or good fortune, and will maximise the chances of hitting targets and achieving objectives. It also demonstrates a more professional approach to colleagues, clients and competitors, who will recognise the value of dealing proactively with all types of uncertainty.

Including opportunity within the definition of risk is not a theoretical or academic exercise driven by a misplaced desire for symmetry. It is a natural consequence of recognising that businesses, projects and people are affected by all sorts of uncertainty, some of which might be helpful if it were managed proactively. Opportunities are important and need to be captured where possible, and the risk process offers a structured way of dealing with them. Doing so delivers genuine practical benefits to the bottom line in terms of increased efficiency and higher success rates.

The real reason for including opportunity within "risk" is because it works!

MINIMISING SURPRISES

It is often said that successful risk management should lead to fewer surprises. Risk management acts as a "forward-looking radar", scanning the uncertain future to identify things that might pose a significant threat to be avoided or an important opportunity to be explored. Even though it may not be possible to discern every last detail of the uncertain future, the risk process aims to expose areas of particular uncertainty and indicate the best path to follow.

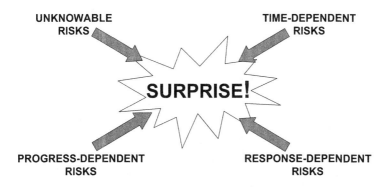

Despite this aim, the future does still contain surprises, both good and bad. Some future uncertainties seem to be unforeseeable. There are four reasons why it is not possible to identify all risks in advance:

1 Some risks are **inherently unknowable**. These are the true unknowns, where uncertainty lurks hidden in the future, unperceived by everyone until it strikes and delivers its surprise impact. In fact it might be true to say that these "unknown unknowns" are not actually risks, since they are essentially invisible to the risk process. It is as if they don't exist until or unless they happen, when they are no longer risks but they are either unexpected problems or unplanned benefits.

2 Other risks are **time-dependent**, and only emerge with the passage of time. The "risk radar" can only see a limited way into the future, and some risks exist below the time horizon. It may not be possible to identify such risks until later on, when they are closer in time. Until they rise above the time horizon they will remain hidden and unidentifiable.

3 Some emergent risks are unforeseeable because they are **progress-dependent**. They cannot be identified until progress has been made. If a risk exists at the back of a building, I cannot discover it until I walk round the building and gain a new perspective. While I am standing in my current position at the front of the building the risk is invisible. Similarly, some integration risks may not be visible until design and development is complete.

4 The last group of risks that can remain hidden from the "risk radar" are **response-dependent**, also known as secondary risks, which only appear when action is taken to respond to an existing risk. Until action is taken these risks do not exist, so of course they cannot be seen before the response is identified.

With so many ways in which risks can be hidden from our forward-looking radar, it seems that risk identification is doomed to failure, since we are unable to identify unknowable risks, emergent risks or secondary risks. This is why risk management is not a single-shot process, but must be repeated on a regular basis. Risk identification should aim to identify **all knowable risks at this point in time**, recognising that some risks are currently hidden from sight. Identifiable risks should be assessed and appropriate actions should be developed.

But the risk process must be iterative, coming back to identify risks that have become visible since the last time. This will include risks that have emerged with the passage of time and as a result of progress made, as well as secondary risks arising from implemented responses.

Unfortunately, risks that are inherently unknowable will always be able to surprise even the most expert user of the "risk radar". But routine updates will minimise additional surprises from risks which are unforeseeable today but which become visible later.

DEALING WITH "UNKNOWN-UNKNOWNS" – THE RUMSFELD FACTOR

Former US Defence Secretary Donald H Rumsfeld will be remembered for many things, not all good. An enduring part of his legacy will certainly be his somewhat garbled comment at the Pentagon news briefing on 12 February 2002: "Reports that say that something hasn't happened are always interesting to me, because as we know, there are known knowns; there are things we know we know. We also know there are known unknowns; that is to say we know there are some things we do not know. But there are also unknown unknowns – the ones we don't know we don't know."

Although this has attracted wide ridicule, careful reading of what he said shows that he is in fact right. And Rumsfeld was not the first to identify the differences between tacit knowledge, explicit knowledge and uncertainty. Confucius is reported as saying, "To know that we know what we know and that we do not know what we do not know – that is true knowledge." Confused yet?? This is all relevant to the world of risk management, because the phrase "unknown-unknowns" (or UNK-UNK) is often used to describe some types of risk.

Both Rumsfeld and Confucius were trying to express something in words which might have been better in a picture, like the one below which maps the presence or absence of knowledge and awareness. In the top right quadrant lies Certainty, where the extent of what is known is fully understood. Below this is the area of Amnesia, representing a blind spot. The top left corner requires Caution, where we are aware of an absence of knowledge. And "unknown unknowns" reside in the bottom left section, with pure Ignorance of the situation faced.

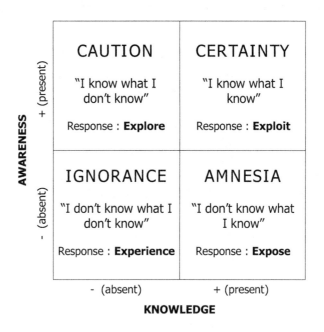

Each zone warrants a different type of response:

- **Certainty** should be **exploited**, playing to strengths and making full use of known facts to take well-founded decisions and actions.

- **Amnesia** needs to be **exposed**, perhaps through a facilitated process, to unlock the knowledge that exists and allow it to be used effectively.

- Areas of **Caution** should be **explored**, seeking to understand the implications of uncertainty or lack of knowledge.

- **Ignorance** can only be tackled through **experiment** or by gaining **experience**, growing in both knowledge and awareness, to reduce the size of this area.

> "To know that we know what we know and that we do not know what we do not know – that is true knowledge."
> Confucius

But which of these quadrants are covered by risk management? If we are concerned about uncertain events that can affect achievement of objectives, then **Certainty** is outside the scope of the risk process. Certain events or circumstances that can affect objectives are either problems (or issues), or benefits. Since all risk is uncertain, risk management is not directly interested in things that are certain (apart from when they cause risk). The **Amnesia** area is also not the direct concern of risk management, since it relates to facts that were once known but are now forgotten (though these might also be causes of risk).

The quadrant where we are aware of a lack of knowledge (the **Caution** zone) is clearly where risk management plays an important role. Here we can explore the boundaries of our uncertainty, and investigate the possible impact on achievement of our objectives. Having understood the scope of the risk, we can develop and implement appropriate responses to manage the risk.

But what about the **Ignorance** area? Can the risk process tackle Rumsfeld's infamous UNK-UNKs? Here's a slightly controversial view – "unknown-unknowns" are nothing to do with risk management! Why might this be true? The reason is philosophical, but the solution is practical.

Philosophically, in concept an unknown-unknown cannot be a risk, as we have already seen. To be a risk managed through the risk process, we have to be able to describe it. If it is truly "unknown" then as far as we are concerned it does not exist, and if it happens it becomes a problem or benefit, not a risk. Unknown-unknowns cannot be managed proactively, only reactively, when they are already outside the scope of the risk process.

So can we do nothing about unknown-unknowns, and are we left to rely on fortune and luck? Fortunately there are two practical things we can do about UNK-UNKs. The best option is to get them out of the Ignorance zone by becoming aware of them, in which case they become "known-unknowns" and fall into the scope of the risk process. Here we need to experiment, learn more about our business, our challenges and constraints. Let's try to find out as much as possible about what we're doing, knowing more and reducing the size of what is unknown. Where this is not possible, we obviously need appropriate contingency and fallback plans – but these are not to manage "the risk", but rather are to cope with the unforeseen impacts of previously unknown events.

Next time someone asks you how your risk process will cope with unknown-unknowns, perhaps you might surprise them by saying it doesn't!

NO RISK? NO CHANCE!

Now we know how to deal with UNK-UNKs. But we still have to face the fact that there's no such think as a zero-risk project. For project-based businesses, risk is a reality, which is why project risk management is essential.

Why are projects always risky? The same factors found in all projects make them inherently risky, including:

- **Uniqueness**, involving at least some elements that have not been done before.

- **Complexity** of various kinds, including technical, commercial, interfaces or relational.

- **Assumptions and constraints** about the future, both explicit (open) and implicit (hidden), which may prove to be wrong.

- **Objectives**, defining the measures by which project success will be determined, which are usually fixed and sometimes conflicting.

- **People**, including project team members and management, clients and customers, suppliers and subcontractors, all of whom are unpredictable to some extent.

- **Stakeholder requirements, expectations and objectives**, which can be varying, overlapping and sometimes conflicting.

- **Change**, since every project is a change agent, moving from the known present into an unknown future.

- **Environment**, including both the internal organisational environment and the external environment where changes beyond control can occur.

These risky characteristics are built into the nature of all projects and cannot be removed. For example, a "project" which was not unique, had no constraints, involved no people and did not introduce change would in fact not be a project at all. Trying to remove the risky elements would turn it into something else. Indeed, projects are undertaken to gain benefits while taking the associated risks in a controlled manner. It is impossible to imagine projects without risk.

Of course some projects will be high-risk, while others have less risk, but all projects are by definition risky to some extent. The "zero-risk project" is an oxymoron – it does not and cannot exist. This of course is why risk management is so important to project success: since all projects are exposed to risk, successful ones are those where that risk is properly managed.

Now that we've looked at some of the key concepts of risk management, it is time to work out how we're going to put these principles into practice so we can achieve our goal of using risk management to lead us to better business. It's time to Make It Happen!

3

Making It Happen – Risk Management in Practice

This chapter provides practical tips and guidance on some aspects of the risk management process that are often misunderstood or poorly performed, with advice on how to avoid common pitfalls.

WHAT'S IN A GOOD RISK PROCESS?

Anyone undertaking a risky or important venture should ask themselves eight simple questions:

1 **What are we trying to achieve?**

2 **What might affect us achieving this?**

3 **Which of those things are most important?**

4 **What shall we do about them?**

5 **Have we taken action?**

6 **Who needs to know?**

7 **Having taken action, what has changed?**

8 **What did we learn?**

These questions describe the steps required to manage risk. They can easily be expanded into a basic risk process, with one process step to answer each question:

1 Getting started (risk process initiation)

Risks only exist in relation to defined objectives, and these are what we are trying to achieve. We cannot start the risk process without first clearly defining its scope and clarifying which objectives are at risk. It is also important to know how much risk key stakeholders are prepared to accept, since this provides the target threshold for risk exposure.

2 Finding risks (risk identification)

Once the scope and objectives are agreed, it is possible for us to start identifying risks, which are the uncertain things that might affect us, including both threats and opportunities. We should use a variety of techniques to help us find as many risks as possible.

3 Setting priorities (risk assessment and analysis)

Not all risks are equally important, so we need to filter and prioritise them, to find the worst threats and the best opportunities. When prioritising risks, we could use various characteristics, such as how likely they are to happen, what they might do to objectives, how easily we can influence them, when they might happen, etc. We might also opt to use quantitative analysis techniques to model overall risk exposure.

4 Deciding what to do (risk response planning)

Once we have prioritised individual risks, we can think about what actions are appropriate to deal with individual threats and opportunities, as well as tackling overall risk exposure. Each risk needs an owner who should decide how to respond appropriately.

5 Taking action (risk response implementation)

Nothing will change unless we actually do something. Planned responses must be implemented in order to tackle individual risks and change overall risk exposure, and the results of these responses should be monitored to ensure that they are having the desired effect. Our actions may also introduce new risks for us to address.

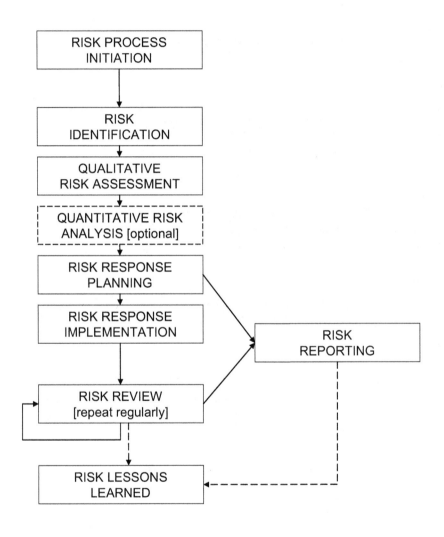

6 Telling others (risk reporting)

Various stakeholders are interested in risk at different levels, and it is important to tell them about the risks we have found and our plans to address them.

7 Keeping up to date (risk reviews)

We have to come back and look again at risk on a regular basis, to see whether our planned actions have worked as expected, and to discover new and changed risks that now require our attention.

8 Capturing lessons (risk lessons learned)

At the end of the exercise we should take advantage of our experience to benefit future similar endeavours. This means we will spend time thinking about what worked well and what needs improvement, and recording our conclusions in a way that can be reused by ourselves and others.

Any good risk process will follow these steps to ensure that we identify, assess and manage our risks effectively. These are not difficult to implement, but without all of these steps a risk process is incomplete.

We will now go through some key aspects of each process step in turn. The aim is not to give a full description of each stage but to highlight areas requiring care and attention.

STEP 1: GETTING STARTED

To get the risk process started, we need to define its scope clearly – clarifying the objectives at risk – and we need to determine how much risk key stakeholders are prepared to accept. This provides the target threshold for risk exposure.

IT'S ALL ABOUT OBJECTIVES

Personal objectives may relate to health, career, family or fulfilment. Objectives for organisations might include growing shareholder value, enhancing customer satisfaction, protecting reputation and operating in a sustainable way. The link between **risk and objectives** is explicit – risk is defined as "uncertainty that matters because if it happened it would affect achievement of one or more objectives." This explains why risk management is so important in all aspects of human endeavour:

- The risk process **requires clearly defined objectives**. It is not possible to define risks without a context. We must first know what is "at risk", what matters, what we are trying to achieve. Only then can we find risks that might affect those objectives. Where objectives are not clear, the risk process forces us to stop and define them before we can go any further.

Risk is defined as "uncertainty that matters because if it happened it would affect achievement of one or more objectives."

- The proactive nature of the risk process **creates management space**, giving us time to think, reflect, and consider the best way to respond. Using the risk process as a forward-looking radar gives us early warning of approaching uncertainties that might affect our ability to achieve objectives.

- The risk process **identifies specific uncertainties** that we can address. This includes both threats that could hinder our progress, as well as opportunities that could help us. By exposing these factors in advance, the risk process gives us a chance to do something about them before it is too late. Where proactive actions are not possible, we have time to decide on contingency plans, or perhaps we might change direction or even stop altogether.

- Prioritising risks by their potential to affect objectives as well as their chance of happening ensures that we **give most attention to the risks that matter most**.

- Properly targeted risk responses should **maximise our chances of achieving objectives**, by removing or reducing a significant proportion of the possible negative effects of threats to our objectives. They should also help us to capture some opportunities and turn them into actual benefits, producing an optimal outcome.

By ensuring that we have clear objectives, making us think in advance about what might affect whether we meet them, identifying the most important risks, and helping us to find appropriate ways of dealing with them, the risk process gives us the best possible chance to succeed in achieving our objectives. This of course is why effective risk management has become recognised as an essential contributor to success in business, projects and other areas of life.

There is one other important implication of connecting risks to objectives in this way. If risk is "uncertainty that matters", it is clear that different things matter to different people, because they have different objectives. Risk does not mean the same to a boss, a middle manager or a front-line worker. It is easy to implement an integrated approach to risk management across an enterprise if there is a coherent and aligned hierarchy of objectives. Risks can be escalated or delegated between organisational levels depending on which objectives are affected. Everyone understands which risks they have to manage at their level in the organisation, because they can just focus on the ones that affect their objectives. Enterprise Risk Management (ERM) depends on having clear objectives across the enterprise.

There is no doubt – when it comes to risk, it's all about objectives!

HOW HIGH IS HIGH?

We know that common definitions of "risk" describe it as an uncertainty that if it occurs would affect one or more objectives. These two dimensions of risk (uncertainty and its effect) are commonly called "probability" and "impact", though other similar terms can be used. Deciding the importance of a particular risk requires assessment of these two dimensions, as well as other characteristics.

The most basic risk assessments often use descriptive labels for probability and impact, such as High, Medium and Low. This would mean that a risk that is not very likely to happen but which would have a major effect if it occurred could be described as "Low-High". While this practice is very common, it can lead to significant misunderstandings. For example if I tell a colleague that one of my risks was assessed as Low-High, she has no way of knowing exactly what I mean. When I say "Low probability", do I mean that the risk has a one-in-a-million chance of happening, or do I use this term to mean <50%? In the same way, does "High impact" mean a total disaster leading to loss of the business, or does it mean a delivery delay of one month?

The usual solution to this potential problem is to define scales for probability and impact for a particular situation, and to insist that all risk assessments of this situation use the same scales. So everyone assessing risks to a specific project might agree that "Low probability" will mean 11–30%, and that "High impact" will mean more than six weeks schedule change or >$1M cost change.

Scale	Probability	+/- IMPACT ON OBJECTIVES		
		TIME	COST	QUALITY
VHI	71–99%	>12 weeks	>$5000K	Very significant impact on overall functionality
HI	51–70%	7-12 weeks	$1000K–$5000K	Significant impact on overall functionality
MED	31–50%	3-6 weeks	$250K–$1000K	Some impact in key functional areas
LO	11–30%	1-2 weeks	$50K–$250K	Minor impact on overall functionality
VLO	1–10%	<1 week	<$50K	Minor impact on secondary functions
NIL	<1%	No change	No change	No change in functionality

This raises a couple of important questions: Who defines the scales, and how?

Definitions of probability and impacts are an expression of the risk threshold or risk appetite for a particular project or business situation. This means that they should be defined by the person who owns the objectives that are at risk. For a project, this means the project sponsor in discussion with other key stakeholders. For a business decision the responsible manager must determine where to set the risk threshold.

This still leaves the question of how to set the numbers. Probability scales are easy to define, by simply dividing the 1–99% range into several sections. Impact is more difficult. Who is to say whether a delay of one month represents a mere inconvenience or a total disaster? Would saving €50,000 be a triumph or just a pleasant surprise?

The process for setting the impact scale for threats is for the responsible person first to decide how much impact would be completely intolerable, describing this in terms of each key objective (for example, time, cost, performance, reputation etc). These values are associated with the top impact scale point (such as Very High). The lowest scale point (for example, Very Low) is addressed next, setting this to a level of impact that is regarded as negligible. Intermediate scale points (for example, Low, Medium etc) can then be set between these outer limits.

Once the threat scales are set, they can be inverted to form scales to be used for assessing opportunities. This simply requires treating impacts as negative for threats (lost time, additional cost, damaged reputation etc), and as positive for opportunities (saved time or cost, enhanced reputation etc). Alternatively an organisation may decide to define specific opportunity scales that differ from threat scales.

Defining probability and impact scales in this way allows everyone assessing risks to use a common framework. My "Low-High" can then be understood by all my colleagues, and it will mean the same as their "Low-High". All the risks within a particular project or business situation will be assessed using the same definitions, allowing us to rank them by their relative importance. This simple definition process answers the question "How high is High?" and makes sure that we are all speaking the same language when assessing our risks.

STEP 2: FINDING RISKS

USE YOUR IMAGINATION

Some say that risk identification is the most important phase of the risk management process, since it is impossible to manage a risk unless it has first been identified. As a result, many risk identification techniques have been developed, including brainstorms, interviews, questionnaires, checklists and prompt lists, assumptions/constraints analysis, SWOT analysis, Delphi groups, nominal group technique, root cause analysis, failure modes analysis and others. Some of these methods are creative and others draw on past experience; some can be undertaken by individuals while others require group input; some approaches are simple and rapid where others are labour-intensive and take time.

Whichever risk identification technique is used however, they all require one factor to make them effective. This powerful characteristic is possessed by all but forgotten by most. Every person is born with it, and some people work to develop theirs into a mature capability while it remains dormant in others. This risk identification tool exists in the human head, and is called the **imagination**.

All risk identification techniques require people to imagine potential future conditions that do not currently exist. The success of risk identification depends on people's ability to envisage imaginary circumstances and possible futures. Without imagination, risk identification is limited to what has happened before, and specific new risks that challenge the current situation cannot be foreseen.

A range of techniques is available to stimulate the imagination, including visualisation, scenario painting, rich pictures, appreciative enquiry, story-telling and other creativity approaches. Risk practitioners should consider using these to develop their own ability to imagine possible risks, as well as to help their colleagues during the risk identification process.

Risk identification requires people to imagine potential future conditions that do not currently exist.

One simple and fun way to encourage the imagination is the use of "fantasy questions" to expose risks in a non-threatening way. These can be employed during risk identification interviews, though they might also be used with other techniques. You can ask yourself, or you can question others. Example fantasy questions might include:

- **If you were dreaming about your business and it turned into a nightmare, what would be happening?**
  (This question encourages people to talk about perceived threats)

- **I am your fairy godmother and you have three wishes to use on your business – what will you do first?**
  (This might result in identification of new opportunities)

- **If an alien joined your management team, what would they find most unusual?**
  (This aims to expose blind spots)

These examples are light-hearted and may not be appropriate for all situations or organisations, but the principle can be applied in a more serious way. Questions can be asked during risk identification interviews that stretch the imagination and encourage the interviewee to consider options beyond their normal experience. For example: "If you were a new employee and this was your first project, what questions would you ask?" "How might this business be different if we were in a foreign country?" "When your client lies awake at night, what is he worrying about?" "What are your supplier's best hopes for this project?"

Questions like these (and other creativity approaches) use the imagination to take us beyond the present and the familiar, opening doors to new possibilities. In a sense all risks are imaginary since they do not yet exist, and imagination-based techniques can be powerful aids to risk identification. If you can imagine something, it could happen. Set your imagination free and see what risks emerge.

> "From the past, the man of the present acts prudently, so as not to imperil the future."
> Titian

PAST, PRESENT AND FUTURE

On a visit to the National Gallery in London, I was struck by one painting in particular – Titian's "Allegory of Prudence". This shows three faces pointing in different directions: an old man (said to be a self-portrait of Titian) looking to the left; a mature man (possibly Titian's son Orazio) facing front, and a younger man (maybe Titian's cousin and heir, Marco Vecellio) gazing right. Below the men are the faces of three dogs positioned in the same way and reflecting the ages of the portraits above them.

Hidden in the dark background above the faces is a Latin inscription: **"Ex praeterito praesens prudenter agit ni future actione deturpet."**

I couldn't resist the challenge of testing my schoolboy Latin, but eventually I needed the gallery's catalogue to help me out. Classically educated readers will already know what Titian was telling us: **"From the past, the man of the present acts prudently, so as not to imperil the future."**

This advice is obviously relevant to managing risk, but it can be particularly useful when thinking about how to identify risks in the first place. Like Titian's painting, risk identification techniques can be divided into three categories with different time perspectives – past, present and future.

1 Historical review techniques

These look at what has already happened in the past, either during this situation, or in others that are comparable. They rely on careful selection of reference points to ensure that they are genuinely similar, and intelligent filtering of data to ensure that only relevant previous risks are considered. In each case, historical review methods ask whether risks that were identified before might arise this time.

2 Current assessment techniques

These involve a detailed consideration of the current situation, analysing its characteristics against given frameworks and models in order to expose areas of uncertainty. Unlike historical review approaches, current assessment techniques do not rely on outside reference points, but are based purely on examination of what exists today.

3 Creativity techniques

There are many risk identification approaches that encourage people to use their imagination to find possible risks that might affect future achievement of objectives. These techniques depend on the ability of stakeholders to think creatively, either individually or in groups, and their success is often enhanced by use of a skilled facilitator.

Each type of risk identification technique has strengths and weaknesses, and no single technique can be expected to reveal all knowable risks. Historical review techniques depend on how relevant previous experience is to the existing situation. Current assessment techniques rely on the quality of the diagnostic process and how well people really understand what is going on. The success of creativity techniques is driven by the ability of participants to imagine the future.

As a result the best solution for risk identification is to use a combination of techniques, perhaps selecting one of each type: past, present and future. For example, it may be best to use a **risk identification checklist** (historical review), together with **assumptions analysis** (current assessment) and **brainstorming** (creativity). It is also a good idea to involve different stakeholders in identifying risks, preferably in groups, as they are likely to see things from a variety of perspectives.

No single technique can be expected
to reveal all knowable risks.

All of which reminds me of another inscription I read once on a greetings card: **"Yesterday is history; Tomorrow is mystery; Today is a gift – that's why we call it the present."** Effective risk identification makes use of all three-time perspectives to give the best possible view of the risks that might affect us going forward into the mysterious and uncertain future.

An organisation or project that relies on a single point of view or only uses one type of risk identification technique is likely to miss important risks, leaving it exposed to threats that could have been avoided, and resulting in missed opportunities. Multiple perspectives offer a broader view of risks that might have an impact, leading to more effective risk identification. As Titian might have said, "that's the prudent way to manage risk."

HOW TO FIND OPPORTUNITIES

Whichever technique we use, the risk process should find and address all sorts of risks, including both negative threats and positive opportunities. Accepting the principle of risk as an opportunity is one thing; using it in practice is another. People who have only used the risk process to identify and manage threats sometimes have problems extending it to deal effectively with opportunities. And the difficulties start right at the beginning: how can we identify opportunities?

The first step is to be clear about what we are looking for: events or circumstances which might or might not occur, but which if they did happen would help us to achieve our objectives; for example, allowing us to work smarter, faster or cheaper.

There are at least four types of opportunity that we should look for:

1   Some opportunities arise from the absence of threats. If the bad thing does not happen we might be able to take advantage of something good instead. For example, if poor industrial relations do not lead to a strike, we might be able to introduce an incentive scheme and turn the situation round from negative to positive.

2   Other opportunities are the inverse of threats. Where a variable exists on a continuous scale and there is uncertainty over the eventual outcome, instead of just defining the risk as the downside it might also be possible to consider upside potential. For example, where the productivity rate on a new task is unknown, it might be lower than expected (a threat), or it might be higher (an opportunity).

3   We should also remember secondary risks, which are introduced by implementing a response to another risk. Sometimes by addressing one risk we can make things worse (the response creates a new threat), but it is also possible for our action to create a new

opportunity. Avoiding potential delays to my car journey by taking the train might also allow me to do some useful work during the journey.

4 Lastly, we must not neglect "pure opportunities" which are unrelated to threats. These are simply unplanned good things that might happen. For example, a new design method might be released which we can apply to benefit our project. Or a new recruit to the team may unexpectedly possess a skill needed to solve a problem. This type of opportunity needs to be actively sought out, requiring fresh thinking and awareness of how potential additional benefits might be created.

Opportunities cannot be managed unless they are identified. People familiar with identifying threats can start with these, then ask whether their absence or inverse might present an opportunity. Planned risk responses should also be examined to see whether they open up new possibilities to help us achieve our objectives. But "pure opportunities" must not be forgotten, since these often present the greatest potential upside of all.

Some worry that proactively seeking opportunities may result in scope creep, as a result of looking for extra unplanned benefits in addition to those already defined in the agreed scope. Pursuing these optional extras might distract attention and effort from the original objectives, and could even be counter-productive. For example, while we are trying to enhance an existing product we might discover a gap in the market for a completely new product. Is this a genuine opportunity to be pursued, or is it just potential scope creep?

To answer this important question, consider how we deal with a threat where the potential negative impact would be outside the scope of a project. We don't automatically take responsibility for addressing this threat within our project, thinking that if we identified it then we should manage it. Instead an out-of-scope threat is (or should be) escalated to someone outside the project who can decide what to do, perhaps the project sponsor or someone in another part of the organisation. In the same way, if we identify an opportunity that is outside the boundaries of our responsibility, we cannot just decide to include it in our project, which would indeed be scope creep. Instead we should escalate the out-of-scope opportunity to someone who is able to decide whether and how to address it.

The only risks which should be managed through a risk process are those which could affect our objectives. Any threat or opportunity where the potential impact is outside the agreed scope should be escalated. This ensures that these types of risk do not automatically result in scope creep – although of course a positive decision could be made to change scope to include a particularly good new opportunity or to avoid a serious wider threat.

BETTER BRAINSTORMING

If you ask people which technique they use to identify risks, most will include brainstorming in the list, usually conducted as part of a facilitated workshop. Indeed for many, brainstorming is not just one technique among several; it's the only one they use. Brainstorming is popular for a range of reasons:

- Everybody feels involved, with an opportunity to share their opinion openly.
- It produces visible results quickly as the flipcharts fill up around the room.
- It's usually conducted in an atmosphere of fun away from the usual workplace.
- It gives people the chance to be creative and "think outside the box".
- It encourages team-building and creates a sense of shared ownership of the output.

But there are some drawbacks to brainstorming that can lead to it becoming ineffective, for example:

- It can be difficult to get the right people to attend, and if key stakeholder perspectives are not present, important risks may be missed.
- The way the group functions can be influenced by groupthink and other subconscious biases.
- Strong individuals can impose their view on the session and inhibit others from contributing.
- The creative non-critical approach often results in identification of other things that are not risks (such as problems, issues, worries etc).

These can be overcome by simple steps such as effective facilitation by someone skilled in managing group dynamics, good preparation by participants before attending the session, and commitment by all to honesty and mutual respect. But even with these in place, brainstorming can run into difficulties.

Part of the problem is that traditional brainstorming was not intended for identifying risks. The technique was originally developed for problem solving, and has two key principles. First is deferred judgement. Idea generation must be separated from evaluation, otherwise the creative flow might be disrupted. Second is that quantity breeds quality. The first idea is rarely the best, so finding more ideas increases the chance of getting good ones. These two principles are expressed in the four rules of brainstorming:

1 Creativity and free thought are welcomed and encouraged, even if they appear unproductive.

2 No criticism is allowed during the session, with judgement being deferred until later.

3 Combination and improvement are sought, to produce better ideas by building upon others.

4 Quantity is required, since more ideas increase the chance of finding a solution.

When brainstorming is used for risk identification, we need to be sure that we identify as many risks as possible from a wide range of sources. Unfortunately the creative process can result in identification of things that are not risks. In addition it is common for a brainstorm session to concentrate on areas where participants are comfortable, such as technical risks, ignoring other important areas such as commercial or external risks. It is also possible for a brainstorm session to go down a blind alley, with people being very "creative" about unrealistic risks (such as an alien invasion, everyone dying from a mystery disease, or the project manager becoming a millionaire).

To avoid these shortcomings, the rules of brainstorming need to be modified when it is used as a risk identification technique. For example it helps to have some evaluation of the ideas initially generated, in order to remove non-risks. Use of a standard risk description (or risk metalanguage) can help to ensure that only genuine risks are captured. It can also be helpful to structure the creativity in a risk identification brainstorm by using risk categories or a Risk Breakdown Structure, to be sure that all possible sources of risk are considered.

Everybody loves brainstorming, but it must be used carefully and intelligently for risk identification if it is to achieve its purpose of allowing key stakeholders to identify as many risks as possible in a creative and fun way.

The rules of brainstorming need to be modified when it is used as a risk identification technique.

ASSUME NOTHING, CHALLENGE EVERYTHING!

When we try to guess what might happen in the future and use that information as a basis for planning or decision-making, we're making an "assumption", and these are an important source of risk, for projects, businesses and life in general.

Making assumptions is a good way of dealing with an uncertain future when there are a number of possible options. It certainly simplifies matters and allows us to get on with things instead of spending a long time analysing all the possibilities. In its most basic form, an assumption is a decision to proceed on the basis that one option will turn out to be correct and others will not happen.

Projects in particular make a lot of assumptions, especially during the planning phase, although most business situations also require us to try to work out what we think is most likely to happen. For example, we might assume that we fully understand the specification and scope, or that our suppliers will deliver on time, or that our client will sign-off all approvals within two weeks, or that all key members of our project team will remain for the duration of the project. But what happens if we assumed the wrong thing? In most cases a false assumption would lead to a problem, since we usually tend to assume that things will go the way we want.

Of course not all assumptions matter equally. There are some assumptions that might prove false without having a significant effect overall, but there are others where a different outcome could be serious.

So we may be assuming that our design team will produce draft designs within a month, but we have enough float in the schedule to cope if it takes two months – the assumption could be false but it wouldn't matter too much. On the other hand, if we make an assumption that regulatory requirements won't change before our product is released into the market, but in fact they do change, then we could be in real trouble. Fortunately there is a simple process for testing how risky our assumptions might be, and for including them in the risk process if necessary. It's called Assumptions Analysis. The first step is to list all the assumptions we have made about our project. A simple IF-THEN statement can be written for each assumption, in the form:

> **"IF this assumption proved to be false,**
> **THEN the effect on our objectives would be ..."**

We can then assess both sides of this statement. On the IF side, we ask how likely the assumption is to be unsafe. Considering the THEN side tells us whether it would matter if the assumption was wrong. Another way of describing this is to see the IF statement as reflecting probability, whereas the THEN phrase is about impact. And probability and impact are the two dimensions of risk. This simple approach can be used to turn assumptions into risks. Where an assumption is assessed as likely to be false and it could have a significant effect on one or more objectives, that assumption should be considered as a candidate risk.

At project level this type of Assumptions Analysis is a powerful way of exposing project-specific risks, since it addresses the particular assumptions made about a given project, rather than considering more general aspects. It is also very useful whenever we have to make a business decision involving significant uncertainty. There are however two dangers with this technique:

1   The first weakness is that this technique can only consider explicit assumptions, which have been consciously made and openly

communicated. There are however many implicit assumptions which we all make every day, some of which are very risky. Assumptions Analysis can't analyse assumptions that remain hidden.

2 Secondly this approach tends only to identify downside risks, threats that a particular assumption may prove false and result in a problem. **Assumptions Analysis is not good at identifying opportunities** because most of our underlying assumptions are optimistic.

The first shortcoming can be overcome by a facilitated approach to identifying and recording assumptions, using someone independent and external to the situation to challenge established thinking. To be fully effective, Assumptions Analysis needs full disclosure.

For opportunity identification, the technique can be extended to address and challenge constraints. These are restrictions on what we can or cannot do, how we must or must not proceed, and they are often imposed from outside, for example by management, clients or regulators. But some of these constraints may not be as fixed as they first appear – indeed some of them might be assumed constraints. In fact it might be possible for a constraint to be relaxed or perhaps even removed completely. Sometimes changing a constraint might not help much, but in other cases it might create the possibility of working more efficiently.

For example, management may have classified your project as low-priority, resulting in inadequate resourcing. But might you be able to get your project reclassified and so gain access to better resources? Or perhaps you've been told that all detailed design must be completed before any implementation can start? If it was possible to relax this constraint to permit parallel development of low-risk elements, that might be very beneficial to the project schedule and save time. On the other hand, if the project end-date coincides with a major product launch event, there may be no schedule flexibility at all. How can we know which constraints are set in stone, and which might be worth changing if possible?

In the same way that assumptions can be tested to expose threats, a similar IF-THEN test can be applied to constraints to identify possible opportunities. This starts by listing the constraints, then writing statements saying:

> **"IF this constraint could be relaxed or removed,
> THEN the effect on our objectives would be ..."**

We are looking for constraints that could possibly be changed (the IF side has a positive probability), and where such a change would be beneficial to achieving objectives (a positive impact on the THEN side). These constraints then present an opportunity where something might be changed in order to promote the achievement of one or more objectives. We can find them through a simple process of Constraints Analysis that matches Assumptions Analysis, but which tests those imposed restrictions to see if any might usefully be challenged.

Instead of making blind assumptions about the future, or accepting that stated constraints are unchangeable, we should be prepared to challenge assumptions and constraints. Asking simple questions about what might happen in the uncertain future can expose significant threats and opportunities, which can then be addressed through the risk process, leading to increased chances of success.

THE DEVIL'S IN THE DETAIL

Risks can be identified and described at different levels of detail, and there can be considerable variation between different projects or organisations. Some projects identify just a small number of high-level risks, while others have many hundreds or even thousands of detailed risks. A generalised or high-level description of risk can make it difficult to develop responses and assign ownership, while describing risks in a lot of detail can create a great deal of work. How can we determine the correct level of detail? There are three components to consider: **management**, **ownership**, and **reporting**.

1 Firstly, risks should be described at the level to which they are going to be **managed**. A high-level description such as, "Something unexpected might happen during the project" is quite useless as no management action is possible at this level. Too much detail is also pointless for example, "George Smith the junior system architect may break his right leg at the football match next Tuesday night and not be able to finish the Phase 2.4.2 detailed design drawings."

The risk might be better stated as, "Key staff may not be available when required to complete the system design." At this level the risk can be managed proactively, with careful resource planning, use of shadowing or deputies, and ensuring that key tasks are not assigned to one person. Of course it is true that some risks will need to be managed at a detailed level while others can be addressed at a higher level.

2 Secondly, each risk should be described at a level of detail where it can be assigned to a single **owner**, with clear responsibility and accountability for addressing the risk. However this also allows for some variation in the level of risk description, as risk owners can range from junior team members who might be responsible for detailed risks, through to senior managers who are only interested in the higher level.

3 Thirdly, the level of risk description should match the **reporting** needs of the person receiving the risk report. Team members need detailed risk descriptions for those risks that they are responsible for managing. The project sponsor or client needs less detail, perhaps with groups of risks being summarised into high-level descriptions.

Each of these three answers suggests that risk descriptions can be useful at various levels for different purposes. There is no one right level that meets all needs. So what can be done?

One useful tool addressing this issue is the Risk Breakdown Structure (RBS), which is a hierarchical structure describing sources of risk. This allows risks to be described at increasing levels of detail. At the top level (Level 0), all risks are simply "Risks". But this can be broken down into major sources of risk at Level 1, such as Technical Risk, Commercial Risk, Management Risk, External Risk. Each of these major areas can be further detailed at Level 2 (for example, Technical Risk could be subdivided into Technology, Performance, Reliability, Interfaces etc). At the lowest level individual risks are described under each specific source. An example RBS is shown opposite.

Different RBS levels can then be used for different purposes. Detailed risk reporting, ownership and management can take place at the lowest level. Higher RBS levels allow groups of risks to be rolled-up and summarised for reporting, ownership and management further up the organisation. So the project safety engineer may need to know about a specific risk affecting a particular product trial (RBS Level 3), whereas the company's Chief Technical Officer may be interested in the overall level of technical risk on a particular project (RBS Level 1).

Risk descriptions at different levels of detail are useful in different ways. Instead of insisting that all risks are described at a single level which may not suit all needs, using a hierarchical RBS can provide the necessary flexibility with both high-level and more detail as appropriate.

RISK BREAKDOWN STRUCTURE		
RBS LEVEL 0	**RBS LEVEL 1**	**RBS LEVEL 2**
0. ALL RISKS	1. TECHNICAL RISK	1.1 Scope definition
		1.2 Requirements definition
		1.3 Estimates, assumptions & constraints
		1.4 Technical processes
		1.5 Technology
		1.6 Technical interfaces
		1.7 Design
		1.8 Performance
		1.9 Reliability & maintainability
		1.10 Safety
		1.11 Security
		1.12 Test & acceptance
	2. MANAGEMENT RISK	2.1 Project management
		2.2 Programme/portfolio management
		2.3 Operations management
		2.4 Organisation
		2.5 Resourcing
		2.6 Communication
		2.7 Information
		2.8 HS&E
		2.9 Quality
		2.10 Reputation
	3. COMMERCIAL RISK	3.1 Contractual terms & conditions
		3.2 Internal procurement
		3.3 Suppliers & vendors
		3.4 Subcontracts
		3.5 Client/customer stability
		3.6 Partnerships & joint ventures
	4. EXTERNAL RISK	4.1 Legislation
		4.2 Exchange rates
		4.3 Site/facilities
		4.4 Environmental/weather
		4.5 Competition
		4.6 Regulatory
		4.7 Political
		4.8 Country
		4.9 Social/demographic
		4.10 Pressure groups
		4.11 Force majeure

STEP 3: SETTING PRIORITIES

Armed with a long list of risks, we now need to prioritise them, to find the worst threats and the best opportunities. Limitations of time and resources mean it is not usually possible to address all risks with the same degree of intensity. We need to undertake Qualitative Risk Assessment.

GET YOUR PRIORITIES RIGHT

A lot of effort goes into prioritising risks, so that an appropriate level of attention can be devoted to dealing with them. Several different parameters can be used to rank risks, although it is common to use just two: probability and impact. Other relevant factors might include urgency, manageability, or response cost etc. People spend a lot of time on prioritisation because they know it is important to concentrate on the biggest risks and avoid wasting effort on small ones. But perhaps we are trying too hard? Maybe a more simple approach to ranking risks would work just as well.

In the health service, resources are often stretched, with insufficient time or funds to treat every patient who asks for help. In situations when doctors cannot examine everyone, it is common to adopt a **triage approach**, first screening all patients to decide which ones need to see a doctor and which can be treated by a nurse. Decisions might be made on the basis of the severity of symptoms or the urgency for treatment. A junior professional often makes the medical triage decision following simple guidelines, dividing patients into two or three groups for further attention.

Businesses working in the energy sector adopt a similar approach to classify oil fields, using the **3P classification** to divide them into three groups. In first group, reserves are **proven** and commercial operations can go ahead with a high degree of confidence. Then there are **probable** reserves, where the chance of recovering oil is less certain but still viable. Finally come the fields classified as **possible**, meaning that oil might be present but there is a high degree of uncertainty over whether it can be recovered commercially.

People spend a lot of time on prioritisation but perhaps we are trying too hard?

These simple prioritisation schemes contrast sharply with the level of detail found in most risk processes. It is common for project teams or managers to argue at length about whether the probability of a particular risk occurring is 10%, 12% or 15%, and to debate whether the most likely impact is $10M or $11M. Even where generic scales are used, people can spend a lot of time disputing between rating a risk as Low or Medium. Perhaps we can learn something from the medical triage approach or the energy sector's 3Ps.

"Simplicity is the ultimate sophistication."
Leonardo da Vinci

It is important to remember the purpose of risk prioritisation. We are not usually trying to obtain a precise estimate of the exact likelihood of occurrence for each risk, or to determine the potential impact against objectives in great detail. Most of the time we are considering a fairly long list of risks, where there are too many risks for us to give them all the same level of attention. We need to divide them into two or three groups, so that we can focus first on those requiring urgent management, then deal with other important risks, and merely monitor the remainder. The use of red-yellow-green "traffic-lights" reflects this broad classification of risks into high-medium-low priority. Separating risks into two or three priority groups does not need complex or detailed ranking schemes. All that is required is to compare risks against a defined threshold and decide whether each particular risk is above or below. In some cases it may be enough merely to rank risks against each other to determine a relative prioritisation, without considering absolute values of probability or impact. We should be careful not to seek more detail than we need for this purpose. If a risk is in the "Top Ten" list it requires urgent attention, and it may not matter whether it is third or fourth on the list. All "red" risks should be treated as high priority and we may not need to worry about whether some are more red than others.

Leonardo da Vinci said, **"Simplicity is the ultimate sophistication."** When it comes to prioritising risks, this is good advice.

PROBLEMS WITH PROBABILITY

Out of "probability" and "impact," which do you think is more difficult to estimate?

It is relatively simple to assess the potential effect that a risk might have on the objectives of a particular project or business, since this merely requires defining the situation after the risk has occurred, and then imagining what might transpire: "If this risk actually happened, then what would the effect be?" Probability is not so easy however. Risk practitioners, management and project teams alike experience repeated difficulty in assessing the probability that a given risk might occur. There are at least four reasons for this.

1. Terminology

In English, different words are often used interchangeably to describe the uncertainty dimension of a risk, such as "probability", "frequency", "likelihood" or "chance". In fact these do not mean the same thing, and confusion can arise if the terms are misused. For example "frequency" describes how often an event or set of circumstances is expected to occur based on previous experience, either in a period of time (e.g. once per year) or in a number of trials (e.g. seven times out of ten).

So frequency really applies to repeatable events. This is not the same as "probability" which is a statistical term describing how likely a single uncertain event or set of circumstances is to occur.

One solution is to use a more general term such as "likelihood", and recognise two variants called "probability" (for single events) and "frequency" (for repeatable events).

2. Format

The uncertainty dimension of a risk can be expressed in several ways, including both numerical and textual formats, such as: 35%, once per month, 2:7, unlikely, one in six times, 10-4, low probability, 0.2, and so on. Most people have problems interpreting and handling different numerical formats, and even the textual phrases can mean different things (as discussed below). This problem can best be overcome by education, as well as using a set of agreed definitions which everyone understands.

3. Subjectivity

Assessment of probability requires forming an opinion about a future event or set of circumstances that have not yet happened. Different people will take different views about the future, and there is no "single right answer" since the future has not yet happened. Risk probability cannot be measured, only estimated.

Assessments of the uncertain future are influenced by many factors, including perceptual filters, motivational bias, cognitive bias, or subconscious heuristics (mental shortcuts). The solution here is to take a team-based approach, exploring different perspectives, examining underlying assumptions, and reaching consensus wherever possible. Sources of bias should also be understood and corrected where possible.

4. Lack of data

Some risks have never been experienced before, especially those relating to the unique aspects of projects or situations of business innovation. In other cases, even though a risk might have been encountered previously, there may be no record of its existence due to absence of a learning mechanism (such as a knowledge base or checklist).

As a result there is no body of evidence to assist in estimating the probability of occurrence of these novel risks. Addressing these shortfalls requires acknowledging that some areas lack relevant previous experience, as well as implementing an effective lessons-to-be-learned process (for example, a post-project review).

One of the most interesting aspects of this problem is the language of probability. There are many English words that could be used to describe how likely something is to occur, and one might imagine that this rich lexicon could help us to be clear. Unfortunately Risk Doctor research has revealed that people attach very different meanings to commonly used phrases such as rare, unlikely, possible or probable. The results are summarised opposite, and show wide variations.

For example "possible" can be interpreted as anything from 29–58%, and "likely" is taken to mean 50–68%. Even "impossible" was used to describe events with 5–11% chance of happening, while "definite" meant considerably less than 100% (77–84%).

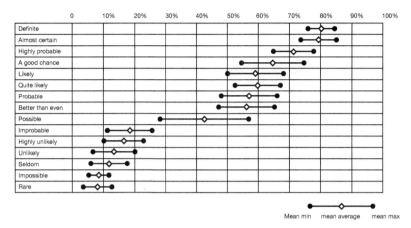

	0	10%	20%	30%	40%	50%	60%	70%	80%	90%	100%
Definite									●─◇─●		
Almost certain								●─◇─●			
Highly probable							●─◇─●				
A good chance						●──◇──●					
Likely					●──◇──●						
Quite likely					●──◇──●						
Probable				●──◇──●							
Better than even				●──◇──●							
Possible			●────◇────●								
Improbable		●─◇─●									
Highly unlikely		●─◇─●									
Unlikely	●─◇─●										
Seldom	●─◇─●										
Impossible	●◇●										
Rare	●◇●										

                          ●────────◇────────●
                     Mean min   mean average   mean max

So there is no doubt that dealing with probability is difficult. But we need to work at this because we cannot properly prioritise risks without considering how likely they are to actually happen. This matters for two main reasons:

- **Faulty probability assessment** means risks will be wrongly prioritised, leading to a failure to focus on the most significant risks, selection of inappropriate responses, inability to manage risks effectively, and loss of confidence in the risk process.

- **Sound assessment of risk probability** improves the understanding of each risk, allowing appropriate prioritisation, better response selection, enhanced risk management effectiveness, and more reliable achievement of project and business objectives.

We need to understand the problems associated with assessing probability, and take action to address the concerns, by using appropriate terminology and formats, identifying and managing sources of bias, learning lessons to improve the effectiveness of the probability assessment process, and monitoring risk management performance to determine the accuracy of assessed risk probability. Properly assessing probability is an essential step in the risk process and it needs to be done with care if the results are to be of any use.

WHAT'S YOUR BIGGEST RISK?

How would you reply if someone asked you, "What is your biggest risk?" It's quite likely that you would be able to answer without too much difficulty, as most of us know what keeps us awake at night, either worrying about what could go wrong (threats), or getting excited about possible improvements (opportunities). But when you answered the question, what criteria did you use? How do you measure the "size" of a risk so that you can determine which is the "biggest"? Is it just an intuitive feeling, or are there measurable parameters we can use?

We have seen how probability and impact are key criteria to consider when deciding how big a risk is, and we've looked at problems with probability. The use of probability and impact as the sole means of sizing risks has led to the supremacy of one technique for prioritising risks in projects. The two-dimensional Probability-Impact Matrix (PIM) is frequently used as the only way to rank risks, combining the two dimensions with top priority being given to high probability-high impact risks. An example PIM is given below, illustrating the typical double "mirror matrix" format that shows both threats and opportunities, with red/yellow/green zones used to indicate high/medium/low priority risks.

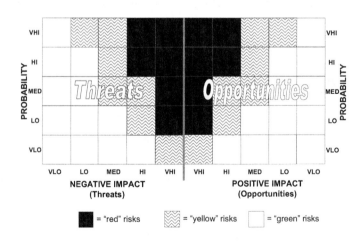

Although the PIM is very common, it is limited by only representing the two dimensions of probability and impact. There are however several other important characteristics of risks which we might want to use when we answer the question, "Which is the biggest risk?" For example:

- **Manageability** – How easy is it to do something about the risk? We may decide that a medium-probability/medium-impact risk that we can do nothing about is more important than a high-probability/high-impact risk that is simple to deal with.

- **Proximity** – If the risk were to happen, how soon would we expect that to be? A risk that might happen tomorrow should be treated as more important than one that might not occur until next month or next year.

- **Propinquity** – How important is the risk to me personally, or to my team/our project/my department? We are more sensitive to risks that affect us directly, and we view risks to others as less important.

- **Urgency** – How much time do we have in order to implement an effective response to the risk? If we must act now to address the risk, we should give it higher priority than one where we have longer to respond.

- **Relatedness** – Is this risk related to other risks? A risk with complex links or dependencies with many other risks should be treated as higher priority than a simple independent risk.

There are other characteristics in addition to these that we might wish to consider when we try to decide how big a risk is, and what degree of priority we should give it. But this list indicates that simply assessing the two attributes of probability and impact is insufficient to answer the question of risk size. The problem is that as soon as we introduce additional criteria into the risk assessment process, the traditional

Probability-Impact Matrix is unable to cope. It is a two-dimensional tool for representing just two dimensions of risk. If we want to include three or more risk characteristics, we need other methods. Fortunately such methods exist, allowing us to prioritise risks in a more intelligent and sophisticated manner. Two common examples include the risk prioritisation chart and the bubble chart, shown below. The example risk prioritisation chart plots probability, impact and urgency, while the bubble chart shows urgency, manageability and impact, but any combination of three dimensions could be used.

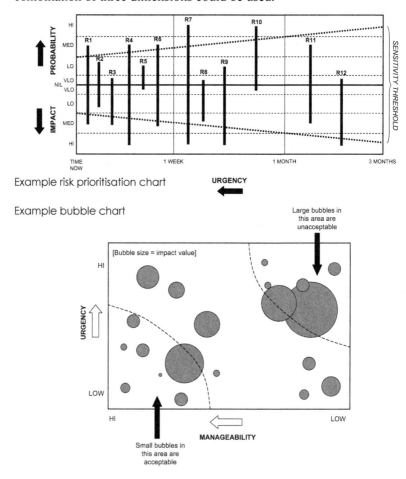

Example risk prioritisation chart

Example bubble chart

Of course the more dimensions you try to use to size your risks, the harder it becomes, both in developing a suitable ranking algorithm and in presenting the results. But the point is that if we try to answer the question, "What is your biggest risk?" by referring only to probability and impact, we are ignoring other important risk characteristics.

It seems unlikely that people will stop using the traditional Probability-Impact Matrix anytime soon, as it is simple and popular. But if we really want to know which are our worst threats and best opportunities, we should use other techniques as well.

IDENTIFYING OVERALL RISK EXPOSURE

We can analyse patterns of risks to elicit useful information about the type of risk exposure we face. Risk identification often produces a long list of individual risks, which can be hard to understand or manage. The list can be prioritised, but this does not indicate those areas that require special attention, or expose recurring themes, concentrations of risk, or "hot-spots" of risk exposure.

There is also often no assessment of overall risk exposure, or of the linkages between risks, either at the same level or aggregated to a higher level. Instead the most common techniques (such as the Probability-Impact Matrix) focus simply on prioritising individual risks, producing ranked lists such as the "Top Ten" risks. Wouldn't it be helpful if there was a simple way of describing the structure of risk exposure?

This is best understood at project level, though the principles apply equally well to other types of risk management. Project management makes wide use of structures, and there are several standard project frameworks, as well as a couple which are specific to risk management. What frameworks are available and can they help us understand risk exposure across a project?

The most commonly used project management framework is the
Work Breakdown Structure (WBS), which divides project work
hierarchically into manageable and definable packages to provide a basis
for project planning, communication, reporting and accountability. Other
common project management hierarchies include the **Organisational
Breakdown Structure (OBS)** and the **Cost Breakdown Structure
(CBS)**. The OBS reflects the management structure of the project,
describing different levels of control, while the CBS provides a basis for
cost estimation, budgeting and control.

On the risk side there are two risk-related frameworks. We have already
seen how the **Risk Breakdown Structure (RBS)** presents a hierarchical
structure of potential risk sources, and can be used in a variety of ways
to structure and guide the risk management process. The **Risk Impact
Breakdown Structure (RiBS)** covers different types of risk impact to
describe characteristics of the risk exposure, and an example is given
below. While both RBS and RiBS apply at project level, these two risk-
based hierarchies can also be used at any level of risk assessment across
the organisation.

RISK IMPACT BREAKDOWN STRUCTURE		
RiBS LEVEL 0	**RiBS LEVEL 1**	**RiBS LEVEL 2**
0. IMPACT ON PROJECT	1. TIME IMPACT	1.1 Project duration
		1.2 Phasing
		1.3 Float
		1.4 Useful product life
		1.5 Obsolescence
		1.6 Interim milestones
		1.7 Delivery schedule
	2. COST IMPACT	2.1 Profitability
		2.2 Margin
		2.3 Cashflow
		2.4 Resourcing
		2.5 NPV
		2.6 ROI
		2.7 Whole-life costs
		2.8 Cost of ownership
		2.9 Liquidated damages
		2.10 Contingency reserve
		2.11 Payback period
	3. SCOPE/QUALITY IMPACT	3.1 Performance
		3.2 Functionality
		3.3 Reliability
		3.4 Maintainability
		3.5 Expansion potential
		3.6 Security
	4. IMPACT ON OTHER OBJECTIVES	4.1 Safety
		4.2 Regulatory compliance
		4.3 Reputation
		4.4 Supply chain
		4.5 Business case
		4.6 ...

How can we use these frameworks to analyse aspects of risk exposure? A variety of different categorisation schemes can be created simply by mapping identified risks into the relevant framework, followed by a summation of either the number of risks, or (better) a weighted sum taking risk severity into account. For example at project level:

- **WBS**
  Mapping risks to the WBS indicates which parts of the project scope are most at risk. The individual work packages containing most risk can be identified, and this can be aggregated or rolled up the WBS framework to find the most risky major tasks, project areas etc.

- **OBS**
  Categorising risks using the OBS shows relates risks to the areas of responsibility of the various individuals, teams or groups in the project organisation, and can be used to propose appropriate risk owners.

- **CBS**
  Linking risks into the CBS allows the cost of risk impacts and planned risk responses to be mapped into the project budget, exposing which cost elements are most uncertain, allowing calculation of an appropriate risk budget, and suggesting where contingency might be required.

- **RBS**
  Grouping risks by the RBS indicates common sources of risk, allowing preventative measures to be taken, and increasing the efficiency of risk responses by targeting root causes to tackle multiple related risks.

- **RiBS**
  Mapping risks against the RiBS allows analysis of the types of risk exposure faced by the project, indicating where the management team should focus attention when developing risk responses.

Clearly each of these categorisations can be used to support risk response planning, ensuring the responses are aimed at the right target, and making best use of the resources available. Simply mapping risks into the various project and risk frameworks provides valuable additional information to assist the project manager in addressing the risk challenge faced by the project.

However, even though these simple classifications are useful, they are still only one-dimensional analyses of the multi-dimensional risk problem area. Cross-framework mapping takes the analysis to another level, providing new insights into patterns of risk exposure. Here are three possible examples:

RBS x WBS
Combining WBS (project scope) with RBS (sources of risk) reveals which types of risks are affecting which areas of the project. Because both WBS and RBS are hierarchies, different levels of analysis are possible, from the top where the whole project is affected by all types of risk, down to lower levels showing particular types of risk faced by specific work packages.

RBS x RiBS
Cross-mapping of RBS against RiBS indicates the combination of sources of risk and potential impacts on objectives. Hotspots within this matrix shows particular cause-effect chains that are significant, and will be useful to support development of effective risk responses. These might be either preventative (targeting common causes of risk) or corrective (addressing common impact areas with fallback plans and/or contingency). As before, this analysis can be conducted at different levels.

RiBS x CBS
Mapping RiBS (types of risk impact) against CBS (cost structure) exposes which types of risk impact are likely to have the greatest effect on the budget, and can be used to develop targeted contingency funds.

The value of this type of mapping lies in its ability to support development of effective risk responses, by revealing different aspects of risk exposure. The use of hierarchical frameworks has an additional benefit in allowing responses to be developed at different levels, ranging from generic responses to detailed specific actions targeting particular hotspots of exposure.

TO QUANT OR NOT TO QUANT?

Risks rarely happen one at a time. Instead they have knock-on effects on each other, with some risks making others more likely and some risks making others impossible. Where qualitative risk assessment studies risks individually, we sometimes need to analyse the combined effect of risks on outcomes, particularly in terms of overall time and cost. This is the purpose of **quantitative risk analysis**.

Quantitative risk analysis is hated by many but loved by some. There are people who say that you can't properly understand overall risk exposure without using a quantitative model. Others say that quantitative risk analysis is too hard, gives misleading results, and is subject to the GIGO effect (garbage-in/garbage-out). Are there any clear guidelines on when quantitative risk analysis is appropriate?

First we should clarify what we mean by "quantitative risk analysis". Strictly speaking this term can be used for any analytical method that uses numbers to estimate the effect of risk on objectives. For most people, quantitative risk analysis means Monte Carlo simulation, but it also encompasses other techniques such as decision trees, influence diagrams, sensitivity analysis, system dynamics, analytical hierarchy process (AHP), fault tree analysis, failure modes and effects analysis (FMEA), multiple estimate regression analysis (MERA), method of moments, and others. First we will focus on Monte Carlo, then go on to look at decision trees, but many of the points apply equally to the other quantitative techniques.

So when should we use quantitative risk analysis techniques? This type of analysis is not suitable for all projects or business situations. Performing a quantitative risk analysis requires additional time and effort that may not be available. Specialist skills may be needed to construct and run risk models, and to interpret the results, and if these skills are not present in-house then they may have to be bought in from expensive consultants. Quantitative risk analysis requires use of specialist software tools, which impose additional costs for purchase, training and maintenance, and which may not interface seamlessly with the existing project management toolset. Quantitative results may not be easy to interpret, and can even be manipulated to give the "right result" by unscrupulous users who may want to support a preferred outcome (for example, to bid or not to bid, or to cancel a project or keep it going, or to support a desired management decision).

For these reasons, people often shy away from using quantitative risk analysis. These techniques are then reserved only for projects and situations that are large, complex, strategically important, mission-critical, sensitive or innovative. Each of these characteristics translates to "high-risk", when a more robust analysis of risk might be justified. However each of the criteria listed above is also subjective and situational. How do you decide if your project is "large" or if your decision is "complex"? Each organisation needs to decide what these terms mean for its business – consequently different organisations will choose to use quantitative risk analysis in different circumstances.

So if you've decided that quantitative risk analysis is appropriate, and that you're going to use Monte Carlo simulation, what do you need to do? There are some prerequisites for a successful analysis, without which you are likely to miss the main benefits.

These include the following:

- A good **baseline model** representing your best plan or base case. This might be a project schedule if you're conducting an analysis of schedule risk, or the cost estimate for a cost risk analysis, or a predicted cashflow for a business investment. For an integrated cost-time risk analysis, a fully costed and resourced schedule is required. If these are very detailed, it may be necessary to produce a summary schedule or estimate to act as a basis for the analysis.

- A **full set of identified risks** which have been assessed for probability and impacts, and which are well understood, including both threats and opportunities. These risks should be clearly documented in the Risk Register, and they will form the basis for the data in the risk model. It is also important to understand any links between risks, including common causes or dependencies, as these will need to be modelled.

- Commitment to **high-quality and unbiased data**, honestly reflecting the effect of risk on planned tasks. It can often be difficult to obtain good risk data, since people wish to present their work in the best light and may be reluctant to admit to any uncertainty. Stakeholders may need help from a skilled facilitator to expose their biases and generate realistic risk data.

- Appropriate **software tools** to perform the analysis, with a good user interface, all the required technical functionality, and the ability to integrate with other management tools. People who can use these tools are also required, able to enter data, generate reports, and interpret outputs.

Assuming that you've covered these prerequisites, what can you expect quantitative risk analysis to deliver? Why bother? These techniques can produce a range of benefits for people who use them properly, including:

- Predicting the combined effect of identified risks on overall outcomes.
- Revealing key risk drivers with the greatest overall influence on the project or business situation.
- Assessing overall risk exposure.
- Testing the likelihood of meeting key objectives.
- Demonstrating the expected effect of planned risk responses.
- Supporting what-if scenario analysis to explore options.
- Allowing determination of appropriate contingency levels.

Quantitative risk analysis should not be avoided or seen as too difficult. It is a powerful technique that offers unique insights into risk exposure. In the right circumstances and used properly, it forms a vital part of the risk toolkit, allowing us to focus on the main risks, and supporting development of effective risk responses.

DECISION TREES

"The future is another country; they do things differently there," to adapt the opening words of L P Hartley's novel "The Go Between". A large part of the risk management process involves looking into the future and trying to understand what might happen and whether it matters. One important quantitative technique that might help is decision tree analysis. This has been neglected in recent years but is enjoying something of a revival. Some people feel it should be reserved for strategic decisions, and others regard the technique as complex and difficult. But at heart it is really quite simple, and can be applied to many different uncertain situations.

The decision tree approach recognises that there are two major factors that affect the future – choice and chance. And in evaluating these we need to consider two parameters – costs and consequences. These four elements form the basis of decision tree analysis.

1   The first step in building a decision tree is to identify the **choices** we must make in trying to achieve our objectives. These choices form the branches of the tree. For example "make or buy", "in-house or out-sourced", "fast-track or traditional", "innovative or proven approach", "supplier A or B", "low or high priority." Each of these decisions leads to different outcomes, which are reflected in the decision tree using the other three elements.

2   The simplest factor associated with alternative choices is **cost**, including both implementation cost and opportunity cost. In some cases this may be negative, reflecting a saving. But it is important to accept that making a choice is rarely a zero-cost action, and an estimate of this must be included against each branch of the decision tree.

3   **Chance** is also an important variable associated with different decision options. Each alternative could have a range of possible outcomes, though some choices could lead only to one certain result. For example different technology options may have different chances of success, or alternative contractors may be more or less reliable. Where there is uncertainty over the result of a decision, this must be identified and assessed, including the estimated probability of each outcome. And some chance events might also open up the possibility of new choices, producing a series of nested branches within the tree.

4   Finally the decision tree must address **consequences**. If a particular decision option were to be taken, incurring both cost and risk, the final result must be estimated, which is usually the payoff for implementing that decision. This is typically expressed in financial terms, though other measures can be used. The decision tree structure describes the predicted outcome of each choice/chance combination, representing the leaves at the end of each branch.

Having built the decision tree from these four components, it can then be analysed to determine the most favourable choice, taking into account the related costs, chances and consequences. First each possible forward path through the tree is followed and its value is calculated by accumulating the costs and payoffs from beginning to end. Then using these path values and working backwards from the end of each branch, the "expected value" of each choice is calculated, taking probability-weighted consequences when chances occur. The branch with the highest expected value becomes the recommended decision option.

Making a choice is rarely a zero-cost action.

There are several challenges in using decision trees effectively, including the practical limitation of the technique to analysing a small number of decision options with a limited range of possible risks. For example decisions trees are of limited use at project level, unless you are looking at a small subset or specific area. The typical project involves many decisions at different levels, each with a wide range of associated risks, and trying to reflect this in a single decision tree could result in a massive and unusable model.

The technique also requires all factors to be represented quantitatively – cost and consequences are usually expressed in financial terms, and probability must be estimated for all chances. And decision tree analysis also assumes a "risk-neutral decision maker" whose choices are based on highest expected value – which is rarely the case.

Despite these limitations, decision tree analysis presents a powerful quantitative technique for assessing possible futures, taking into account the effects of both choice and chance and estimating both costs and consequences.

STEP 4: DECIDING WHAT TO DO

Now we need to think about appropriate actions to deal with individual threats and opportunities, with an owner for each risk – someone who can make a difference and decide how to respond.

THINK STRATEGICALLY

Three things are essential if risk management is to work: first, we must realise that every project, programme, business decision and enterprise is affected by risk, but that risk can be managed proactively; second, we need a process to filter and prioritise risks for further attention; third, we must act.

Unfortunately, after assessing their risks, many people stop, believing that knowledge will protect them. However awareness and assessment do not change risk exposure, unless they lead to action. This is why every risk management process includes a step where responses to risks are developed and implemented. Only then can threats be avoided or minimised, and opportunities can be exploited or enhanced.

Risk metalanguage can provide a framework for development of appropriate responses to both threats and opportunities, ensuring that actions effectively achieve the desired results. In order to understand a risk fully it is helpful to identify its causes as well as its effects. Risk metalanguage can help by separating cause-risk-effect in a three-part description such as, "Because of <one or more causes>, <risk> might occur, which would lead to <one or more effects>." This structured description not only ensures clear definition of the risk, but can also be useful when developing responses.

There are four basic types of risk response:

1 Aggressive responses, either to **avoid** a threat by making it impossible, or to **exploit** an opportunity by making it definitely happen.

2 Involving a third party to manage the risk, either **transferring** a threat, or **sharing** an opportunity.

3 Changing the size of a risk, tackling probability and/or impact to **reduce** a threat or **enhance** an opportunity.

4 Taking residual risks which cannot be managed proactively or cost-effectively, **accepting** either a threat or an opportunity.

Each of these strategies can be linked to the cause-risk-effect structure. For threats (such as, risks with negative impacts) this means the following:

- **Avoidance** can be achieved by removing or changing a **cause**, or by breaking the **cause-risk link** so that the threat is no longer possible. For example risks arising from lack of expertise might be avoided by outsourcing or partnering. Exchange-rate risk might be removed by using only local currency.

- **Transfer** tackles the **risk** itself, by involving others in its management, though it does not change the risk directly. Insurance is the classical example of threat transfer, though contract terms can also be used.

- **Reduction** targets the probability of a threat by seeking to weaken the **cause-risk link**, or aims to minimise negative impact by addressing the **risk-effect link**. For example, knowing that use of a new supplier creates the risk of misunderstood requirements, familiarisation workshops can be held to make this less likely.

- **Acceptance** focuses on the **effect**, recognising that some threats are not controllable and might happen. This strategy might simply involve setting aside contingency funds to recover from negative impacts, or could involve developing a specific fallback plan to be implemented if we were unlucky and the threat occurred.

Similar thinking applies to opportunities (such as, risks with positive impacts):

- **Exploit** the opportunity by leveraging its **cause** so that the opportunity is realised. For example a positive decision might be taken to include an optional item in the scope of a project to create additional benefit.

- **Sharing** an opportunity addresses the **risk** part of the cause-risk-effect chain, by getting others involved in managing the opportunity, perhaps through a risk-sharing partnership or incentivised contract.

- **Enhancing** requires either strengthening the **cause-risk link** to increase the probability that the opportunity will occur, or reinforcing the **risk-effect link** to maximise its positive impact. If attending a trade show creates the opportunity for new business, action can be taken to maximise visibility and attract contacts.

- **Accepting** that an opportunity cannot be influenced proactively means that attention is focused on its **effect**. Contingency funds might be allocated to take advantage of positive impacts, or a specific fallback plan could be developed for use if we were lucky and the opportunity happened.

THE SEVEN As TEST

The risk response planning phase is where we get the chance to make a difference to the risk exposure of our project or business. If we design and implement good risk responses to address the risks we have identified and assessed, we will be able to minimise threats and maximise opportunities, and so optimise the likelihood of achieving our objectives. But if our risk responses are ineffective (or not implemented), the level of risk exposure remains unchanged – or may even get worse!

When designing responses to risks, whether threats or opportunities, it is important to consider whether they will have the desired effect. How can we ensure that we develop the best possible responses? How can we know that our planned responses will work? The following "Seven As" criteria can be used to test whether your planned risk responses are likely to work.

To be effective, all proposed risk responses should be:

1 Appropriate
We need to choose the correct level of response, based on the "size" of the risk. This ranges from a crisis response where we cannot proceed without the risk being addressed, through to a "do nothing" response for

minor risks. In some cases it might be entirely appropriate to stop until a particular risk has been dealt with, and other risks can be completely ignored. Clearly it is vital to distinguish between these two categories, so that major threats or opportunities are not ignored while we waste valuable time and resources on tackling minor ones.

2 Affordable

We must determine the cost-effectiveness of responses, so that the amount of time, effort and money spent on addressing the risk does not exceed the available budget or the degree of risk exposure. Each risk response should have an agreed budget that is affordable within our overall budget.

3 Actionable

We must identify the action window within which responses need to be completed in order to address the risk. Some risks require immediate action, while others can be safely left until later. It is important to identify whether action is possible in a timeframe that allows the risk to be tackled effectively.

4 Achievable

There is no point in describing responses that are not realistically achievable or feasible, either technically or within the scope of our capability and responsibility. For example, the threat of reduced productivity rate might be tackled by a proposed response to cancel all holidays and enforce weekend working; however if this is not possible given working terms and conditions, the response is useless. Similarly a response to capture the opportunity of including additional functionality by immediately recruiting ten world-class engineers to the team can probably not be implemented.

5 Assessed

We need to be confident that all proposed responses will work and be "risk-effective". This is best determined by making a predictive "post-response risk assessment" of the risk assuming effective implementation of the response, and comparing this with the "pre-response" position. For threats the aim is to decrease probability and/or impact, whereas these should be increased for opportunities. We should also predict the level of residual risk (such as, what remains after planned responses have been implemented).

6 Allocated

There should be a single point of responsibility and accountability for implementing the response. It is important to nominate a response owner for each response, who will be accountable for its implementation, although they may choose to delegate actions to others. It is recommended that each response should have a single owner to focus this accountability.

7 Agreed

We must obtain the consensus and commitment of stakeholders before agreeing responses. It is particularly important to gain the buy-in of response owners who are expected to implement planned actions, so that responses are not imposed on people who are unwilling or uncommitted. One way of maximising buy-in is to involve proposed response owners in development of the response.

Each proposed response should be tested against these seven criteria before it is accepted for implementation, to ensure that it is likely to be effective and achieve the intended result. Risk management will never deliver the promised benefits unless effective risk responses are both planned and implemented. Testing our proposed risk responses against the "Seven As" criteria will maximise their effectiveness and ensure that we can properly tackle the inevitable risk exposure on our projects.

Now we have decided what to do, we need to implement our risk responses.

STEP 5: TAKING ACTION

However clever our plans, nothing will happen unless we actually put them into action. It's time to jump to it.

GET THE FROGS OFF THE LOG

Which is the most difficult step in the risk management process? Where do most businesses and projects fail to gain the benefits of their attempts to manage risk proactively? If your organisation is typical, there's one particular step where it all seems to go wrong, and the risk management process becomes just another frustrating hoop to jump through, with no tangible benefits.

So, is it the initial **risk process initiation** step, defining objectives and setting context and scope? Although many make the mistake of trying to start identifying risks without first defining their objectives, this initiation step is not inherently difficult. With **risk identification** it's vital to ensure we identify risks, and not related non-risks (for example, causes, effects, problems or issues), but this step is usually OK.

Prioritising risks using **qualitative risk assessment** techniques to estimate probability and impact is straightforward and, although **quantitative risk analysis** using simulation techniques may seem technically difficult to the non-expert, there are good user-friendly risk analysis tools to help. How about **risk response planning**? Given a structured approach to response development, this shouldn't pose too many problems if the risks are well understood.

What comes next? Is the risk process complete when responses have been agreed? This is the point where **analysis** needs to be turned into **action** if the risk process is to influence risk exposure. The process so far has just provided information about the risks we are facing, but identification, assessment, analysis and response planning do not actually affect the risks. Only action can make a difference.

And it is precisely at this point where most organisations allow their risk process to falter, without making the vital transition from plans to actions. If risk responses are not implemented proactively and effectively, the risk process will be a waste of time, since nothing will change.

This dilemma can be illustrated by a well-known riddle:

There are five frogs sitting on a log, and four decide to jump off. So how many frogs are on the log?

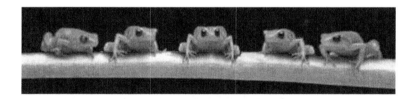

Of course the answer to the riddle is ... **five**. There are still five frogs on the log, because **there's a big difference between deciding and doing!**

And if the risk process ends with risk response planning, with merely deciding what could be done about each risk, but doesn't go on to implement those plans, the frogs are still sat on the log. So how can we **get the frogs off the log?**

A few simple steps will ensure that risk responses become more than just wishful thinking or good intentions, but that instead they are translated into effective action:

1   Make sure that each risk response has an agreed owner to be responsible & accountable for its execution.
2   Allocate realistic durations, budgets and resources to each agreed risk response.
3   Add agreed risk responses to the plan as new activities.
4   Monitor each risk response like any other activity, reviewing & reporting progress etc.

Of course it is vital to go through the earlier stages of the risk process, to identify risks, assess their significance, plan responses and decide actions. But risk cannot be managed unless "deciding" is turned into "doing". So next time you finish planning how to respond to your risks, remember to go the next step, leap into action, and **get the frogs off the log!**

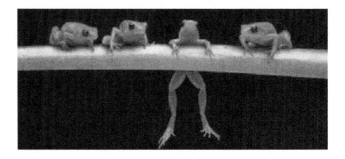

TURNING PLANS INTO ACTION

The risk management process is not difficult, because it is just a structured way of dealing with uncertainty that matters. All you need to do is determine which objectives are at risk, then identify uncertainties that might affect their achievement. The next step is to prioritise identified risks and decide how to respond, and then take action. But although this process is simple to describe, it seems hard to make it work in practice. And the hardest part of all is the last step – risk response implementation.

For some reason, we seem well able to identify and assess risks, and to devise appropriate responses. The problem arises with putting our plans into action. Why does this happen?

A common problem is lack of time or effort for risk response implementation. Many of us are so busy doing our normal tasks that we have no time to do the extra work involved with risk responses. But if we are "too busy to manage risks", then we are "too busy". Since risks by definition are uncertainties that if they occurred would affect achievement of our goals, then addressing them is essential. Risk responses are not "optional extras".

> Identifying risk responses but not doing them is a complete waste of time.

Removing threats and capturing opportunities should be part of our normal job as we seek to maximise our chances of success, not additional tasks to perform "if we get time". Many individuals and teams identify and assess risks, develop response plans and write a risk report, then "file and forget". Actions are not implemented and the risk exposure remains the same.

We can overcome this barrier by treating agreed risk responses as normal work, with the same priority as pre-planned tasks. This will encourage people to implement them: when response owners realise that these actions are important to success, and that risk responses will be treated as legitimate tasks, then they will give them the same degree of attention and effort as their other work. After all, identifying risk responses but not doing them is a complete waste of time. Only when we put agreed responses into action can we change the risk exposure and improve our chances of meeting our goals.

STEP 6: TELLING OTHERS

WHO NEEDS TO KNOW?

Einstein is reported to have said: **"The major problem in communication is the illusion that it has occurred."** Communication is a two-way process, involving both send and receive. I may think I am sending a clear message to you as I write a note, but unless you receive it and understand what I meant, I have failed to communicate with you.

We can't simply give everyone a copy of the Risk Register and expect them to deduce the information they need.

It is very important to give proper attention to how we communicate about risk, to ensure that people have the information they need in order to respond appropriately.

One problem with risk communication is that there are many different people who need to know about risk, but they do not all need the same information. We can't simply give everyone a copy of the Risk Register and expect them to deduce the information they need. Communicating about risk deserves more care and attention than that.

Different stakeholders need different levels of risk information. A **stakeholder** is defined as any person or party who has an interest in success. This includes the sponsors, managers, project teams, customers or clients. It may also include suppliers, subcontractors, users, senior managers, joint venture partners, the general public, regulators, politicians, pressure groups, and even competitors. How can we decide what to tell each of these very different groups of people?

There is a simple answer to the question of what risk information should be provided to each stakeholder. It relates to the level of their interest, or their "stake". The risks should be reported at the same level as their stake. So:

- The project team need to know about detailed project risks in their area of the project.
- Managers need to know about all risks to objectives under their remit.
- A sponsor is interested in business benefits and deliverables, so needs to know about risks to these.
- Users need to know about functionality risks.
- Senior management should be told about strategic risks.
- And so on …

Each risk is defined in relation to an objective, and objectives exist at different levels in the organisation. The stakeholder who is either responsible for a particular objective or interested in its achievement needs to know about any associated risks.

A range of outputs from the risk process should be designed, with the following considerations:

- **Content**
  A range of risk outputs can be produced at different levels of detail, designed in a hierarchical manner, so that high-level outputs can be produced as summaries of more detailed reports, in order to avoid the overhead of producing multiple outputs.

- **Delivery method**
  Alternatives might include written reports in hard copy or electronic format (email, intranet, website, accessible databases), verbal reports (briefings, presentations, progress meetings), graphical or numerical outputs (tables, charts, posters) etc.

- **Responsibilities**
  Each output needs an owner responsible for its production, and an approval authority. It may also be helpful to identify those whose contributions will be required, and who will receive the output for information. A RACI Chart might be useful to define and document this (Responsible, Approver, Contributor, Informed).

Each stakeholder who is either responsible for a particular objective or interested in its achievement needs to know about any associated risks.

Some stakeholders might require only a copy of the current Risk Register, or an extract of relevant data from it. Others might need the Risk Register plus an explanatory narrative, or a full risk report. A summary report might suit other stakeholders who do not require the full detail. In some cases a simple graphical output or dashboard might be appropriate.

As each stakeholder has a different requirement for risk-related information, the risk process should recognise this and deliver timely and accurate information at an appropriate level of detail to support the needs of each stakeholder. When all stakeholders get the information they need from the risk process, they will be able to play their part in ensuring that risk is properly managed.

STEP 7: KEEPING UP TO DATE

THE RISK REAR-VIEW MIRROR

If risk management was looking for a patron, a good choice would be Janus, who was the two-faced Roman god of doorways, looking both back at the way he had come and forward at what lay ahead.

Risk management is of course about looking forwards, scanning the uncertain and unclear future in an attempt to discern what awaits us. It offers businesses, projects and individuals a "forward-looking radar", identifying threats to be avoided and opportunities that might be captured. Even though the precise details of such uncertainties may remain unclear, the "risk radar" can make us aware of their location and size, helping us to formulate appropriate action plans in advance. Most of the risk identification techniques discussed in Step 2 are forward-looking implementations of this "risk radar", and we're quite familiar with the idea of scanning the future to find risks.

But what about the other direction, the "rear-view mirror"? Having taken action to address identified risks, we need to review what has changed, looking again at risk on a regular basis, because risk poses a dynamic and changing challenge to a business.

Strictly speaking there is no risk in the past, since it has already occurred (although we may remain uncertain about what actually happened and what it means!) But as the Spanish satirist Jorge Santayana observed in 1905: **"Those who cannot remember the past are condemned to repeat it."** So we must review the past in order to learn for the future. Then we can update risk identification tools such as checklists, incorporate preventative risk response strategies into the future, and improve the effectiveness of risk management. It might also be possible to estimate return on investment (ROI) for the risk process, by comparing specifically attributable benefits with process costs.

If we do not learn lessons from our past, we will repeat it. People often say: "This risk always affects us, and it usually happens!" The first time I heard someone say that, I reacted instinctively and told them that I considered it very unprofessional for them to allow the same risk to keep happening. My view is summed up in this Risk Doctor proverb:

> **If a risk happens once, that's understandable;**
> **If the same risk happens twice, that's unlucky;**
> **If the same risk happens three times, that's unacceptable.**

Of course it is in the nature of risk to be uncertain, and sometimes risks occur even to the best risk manager. So we can understand it if a risk may occasionally occur, despite implementation of a full range of risk management efforts. And if the same risk should happen a second time in the same circumstances, then that might just be a result of bad luck and not necessarily due to bad management. But if a risk occurs a third time then something is wrong. Perhaps there is a systemic weakness that exposes the organisation or project to the same risk repeatedly. Or maybe the individuals and team have a blind spot where they consistently fail to see a particular risk. Or a routine procedure or process may be flawed and produce the same risk every time it is executed.

This saying applies particularly to negative risks (threats), where it is a bad thing if they happen. However the same idea is also true for positive risks or opportunities, where it is understandable if a single specific opportunity is missed, but we should not allow that to be repeated. In this case the phrase **"risk happens"** in the Risk Doctor proverb should be replaced with **"opportunity is missed."**

As we focus on the challenges ahead, we must also remember our past, learn the lessons from our journey to this point, and not repeat the same mistakes.

STEP 8: CAPTURING LESSONS

DON'T MAKE THE SAME MISTEAK TWICE

Companies obviously aim to generate deliverables that will create benefits and value as defined in each business case, but another aim should be to increase organisational learning. Learning lessons creates a body of knowledge and experience on which we can draw in order to carry out future business more successfully. Unfortunately this aspect is missing from many organisations, and as a result they deny themselves a major source of potential benefits.

Lessons-learned reviews are often badly performed for at least three reasons:

1 Organisations tend to disband teams immediately after a major business initiative or project is completed, moving staff on before they have a chance to capture their knowledge and experience in a structured and usable way.
2 In a cost-constrained environment, reviews can be seen as an optional luxury.
3 Many organisations lack the knowledge management infrastructure to take advantage of previous experience, and feel that there is no point in recording information that is never used.

Outputs from this type of review are usually called "lessons learned". Unfortunately this may be overoptimistic, as lessons are only truly learned when they have been implemented next time around. As a result, it might be better to call these either "lessons identified" or "lessons to be learned".

One important area is identification of risk-related lessons. Organisations need to avoid making the same mistakes twice, either in terms of being hit by problems that could have been foreseen as threats, or missing benefits that could have been spotted as opportunities. Risk elements should be considered in a structured way.

Lessons are only truly learned when they have been implemented next time around.

We've seen the value of a generic Risk Breakdown Structure (RBS) to help us consider all sources of risk (Step 2) and find patterns of risk exposure (Step 3). The RBS has one more useful function at the end of the risk process: it can act as a framework to ensure that all sources of risk are considered during the lessons-learned review, and to provide a comparative structure for transferring lessons. For each element of the RBS in turn, ask these questions:

- What were the main risks identified (both threats and opportunities)? Do any of these represent generic risks that might affect similar projects or business situations and decisions?
- Which foreseeable threats actually occurred, and why? Which identified opportunities that could have been captured were missed, and why?
- Which issues or problems occurred that should have been foreseen as threats? Which unplanned benefits arose that should have been identified as opportunities?
- What preventative actions could have been taken to minimise or avoid threats? What proactive actions could have been taken to maximise or exploit opportunities?
- Which responses were effective in managing risks, and which were ineffective?

- How much effort was spent on the risk process, both to execute the process, and to implement responses?
- Can any specific benefits be attributed to the risk process, e.g. reduced project duration or cost, increased business benefits or client satisfaction etc?
- Where any elements of the risk process particularly effective or ineffective? How could the process have been improved (including tips and hints on using the various tools and techniques)?

The results from this review should produce a range of recommendations including:

- Risks to be added to the organisation's risk checklist, for consideration during the risk identification step for future similar projects or business.
- Modifications to the Risk Breakdown Structure, if risks were identified which did not map into the existing RBS framework.
- Proactive and preventative actions to be included in the strategy for future similar situations to address the types of risks likely to be encountered.
- Changes to the risk process to improve effectiveness, either in use of tools or techniques, or in development of standard templates to support the process.

Just as the post-project review is intended to be a vital closing part of the project management process, in the same way it is essential that risk-related lessons are recorded at the conclusion of every risk process so that reusable knowledge and experience is not lost to the organisation.

We should challenge anyone who says: "The same risk keeps happening all the time." If we identify an event or set of circumstances that always occurs on every project or which happens every time we encounter the same situation, then we need to question whether this is in fact a risk at all.

All risks are uncertain, which means that they may or may not happen. If it is not uncertain then it is not a risk. Events or conditions that always occur should be treated as facts and our standard operating procedures should take them into account. We should not be surprised by something that "always happens" and we should be ready to deal with it, building a response into our baseline plan, learning from previous similar experiences, and being prepared to tackle repeated threats or capture recurring opportunities.

We should challenge anyone who says: "The same risk keeps happening all the time."

GIGO – DRAWING THE RIGHT CONCLUSIONS

The term GIGO is famous as an abbreviation for the phrase "Garbage In Garbage Out." Originally used in the IT industry, it described the fact that the output from a computer system was only as good as its input. Even the best programme cannot take meaningless data and produce meaningful results. Of course GIGO applies much more widely than just computers. The integrity of the output from almost every system or process depends on the integrity of its input – with the possible exception of the human brain, which seems able to create order out of chaos by the application of reasoning and intelligence (at least sometimes!). And "Garbage In Garbage Out" can certainly apply to the risk management process.

The Risk Doctor variant on GIGO translates it as "Garbage In Gospel Out". This describes the tendency of people to accept output from a system without judging it critically. Even if the input is rubbish, we still believe the result, usually because we don't fully understand the way the system works to produce it. This is sometimes called "blind faith."

"Garbage In" to the risk process can mean lack of agreed objectives, poor or lazy risk identification, or use of inappropriate risk responses. "Gospel Out" means treating outputs as infallibly true, with no need for interpretation or judgement.

There is of course a third meaning for GIGO – "Gospel In Garbage Out" – where the system takes good data but introduces errors or makes wrong calculations, and so produces nonsense results. In the risk process this often arises from lack of time, attention or resources for risk management, the use of inappropriate tools or techniques, or lack of risk skills.

How can risk management avoid these three GIGO problems? The third is perhaps easiest to address, since "Gospel In Garbage Out" can be avoided by using a sound risk process, together with staff training and proven tools.

Both "Garbage In Garbage Out" and "Garbage In Gospel Out" can be tackled by applying two filters to the risk process:

1 Verify the input
This means asking questions about the data fed into the risk process. Is it complete? Is it up to date? Can we trust it? Is it influenced by bias, assumptions or a limited perspective? Is it accurate? Is it relevant? And most importantly – is it true?

2 Validate the output
Here we are checking the results of the risk process to see if they make sense. Do the outputs match expectations (and if not, why not)? Are they counter-intuitive (and if so, why)? Is there a clear trend from

previous results? Can we double check using other approaches? And can we act on the results with confidence?

Of course verification is not a simple task because input to the risk process is inevitably uncertain. It involves subjective judgements about what the risk is, how likely or severe it might be, and what responses are appropriate. But we should still ensure that input data quality is as high as possible.

And although risk outputs may sometimes be surprising or counter-intuitive, they should always make sense if the underlying risk process is sound. We should not be afraid to challenge assumptions and test outputs before we use them as a basis for decisions and actions.

So verifying input ("Is it true?") and validating output ("Does it make sense?") can protect against the perils of GIGO. These dangers are real but they can be overcome, and they should not stop us from using risk management on our projects or in our business. After all, there is one thing worse than GIGO, and that is NINO: "Nothing In Nothing Out"!

FLEXIBILITY – THE KEY TO SUCCESS

I recently travelled to London by train. We left the station at the scheduled time, followed a fixed route, stopping at a number of predetermined stations on the way, and arrived in London two minutes early. I also recently took a trip on a sailing boat across a small bay. Following a short delay in getting the boat ready, we set off in the right general direction, but were soon driven off course by the wind and tides. We also had to avoid other boats during the crossing, as well as one fast-moving jet-ski that appeared unexpectedly in front of us. Fortunately we were able to reach the other side by adjusting the sails and steering the boat carefully. Our route was certainly not a straight line across the bay, but we arrived at our chosen spot close to the expected time (and we had a very enjoyable time on the way!)

Which of these two journeys best represents your project or your business? Are you travelling by train or sailing a boat? Do you follow a set plan and schedule, expecting each milestone to be passed on time, and hoping to arrive at your destination exactly when you planned (or at least reasonably close)? Is your motto "Plan the work, then work the plan"? Or are you affected by events and circumstances (both foreseeable and unplanned) that require corrections en route to ensure that you arrive safely?

Most of us recognise that life, businesses and projects do not follow straight lines. In most cases, we can set clear goals, and we are often able to plan a route to get us there. However we know that reality is nearly always more untidy than our neat plans. Risk management is one response to this situation, seeking to look ahead and identify possible sources of variation to the plan, then developing appropriate actions to keep us on course.

However even risk management is difficult if you try to run your project or business like a train journey. You have to stay on the fixed rails that lead from start to finish, follow the published timetable, and no deviation is possible. If unexpected events occur (such as fallen trees on the line, or a passenger is taken ill), delay or cancellation are the only options. It would be far better to treat projects and businesses like sailing boats. Their key characteristic is **flexibility**, the ability to respond quickly to changing circumstances. If the wind blows us off course we can adjust our sails to stay heading towards our goal, and we can even use the wind to assist us on the way.

Of course train and boat journeys are just analogies or similes, which must not be stretched too far. But businesses and projects have to operate in changing environments, where it might not be possible or desirable to stick to the original plan. We need built-in flexibility to allow us to alter course rapidly when things around us change. We should not be rigidly restricted to "staying on track" or trying to avoid "coming off the rails". Instead we should be free to take advantage of change in order to avoid or minimise threats, exploit or maximise opportunities, and so achieve our goal.

How can businesses and projects ensure that they remain flexible? This starts with a management mindset and organisational culture that accepts uncertainty and does not demand unthinking adherence to "The Plan". Good plans should include appropriate levels of contingency or reserve, to respond to emergent threats and opportunities. Processes must allow people to respond to changes as they arise, and should not form a straitjacket that imposes conformity. There must of course be a clear vision and a firm focus on the intended goal. The organisation must also have the ability to know where it is and where it's heading. Finally people should be empowered to act quickly within clear boundaries of authority and accountability, so that they can act appropriately when things change.

So next time someone asks whether your business or project is "on track", why not reply that you are "navigating towards the goal", with a clear view of where you are going and a flexible approach to respond to whatever happens along the way.

Having masterminded the key steps of the risk management process in practice, in our next chapter we need to throw a potential spanner in the works by considering the impact of one very important factor – people!

4

The P-Factor – People

Computers, robots, machines, formulae, techniques, tools or processes do not manage risk. Risk is managed by people making judgements, decisions and choices in the face of uncertainty as they see it. Unfortunately different people see the same risk differently, and this has a huge influence on how they behave towards it. Some will feel driven to caution, afraid of what might go wrong. Others might react more positively, hoping to exploit risk to their benefit.

Different perceptions are not right or wrong, just different. But if we rely on tools and techniques, systems and processes and fail to understand the people aspects of managing risk, we will have limited success. The right approach is not "either/or" but "both/and." We need to take risk psychology into account as we execute our risk processes if we want to manage risk effectively.

While the Three Ts – Tools, Techniques and Training – are important, they are not the whole story. An effective risk process is necessary but not sufficient: it exists to allow risk to be managed. And management of risk is only achieved by people actually using the results of the risk process to inform and modify their decisions and actions. Many factors affect the extent to which people are prepared to use risk results in practice, and these need to be understood and managed if risk management is to fulfil its promise and deliver improved performance.

In this chapter we will explore the P-Factor, the human side of risk management. We will focus on why some people are risk-averse while others are risk-seekers, how risk attitude affects their judgement and behaviour, and what we should do about it.

Different perceptions of risk are not
right or wrong, just different.

TEN KEY CONCEPTS

Risk psychology is a complex area, with a lot of academic research and many textbooks. However there is not much practical advice available for people who are interested in making good decisions in their personal lives and at work. Our long-standing collaboration with Ruth Murray-Webster has resulted in some useful and practical insights into the area of risk attitudes and we have distilled our thinking into **ten key concepts**. (You can find out more about this collaboration at www.risk-attitude.com.)

These ten concepts start from our basic understanding of the nature and characteristics of risk, and move through the main conclusions from our work on applied emotional literacy, to a final statement that explains why it is important to understand and manage risk attitudes if we want to **promote appropriate risk-taking**. The first five concepts (1–5) cover the basic fundamentals of risk management that we have already discussed, and the second five concepts (6–10) move into the area of risk attitudes.

1 **Risk is "uncertainty that matters"** – but different things matter to different people to a different extent in different circumstances.
2 **Risk includes both downside (threats) and upside (opportunities)** – both types of risk need to be addressed proactively, in order to minimise threats and maximise opportunities.
3 **"Zero risk" is unachievable and undesirable** – all aspects of life (including business and projects) involve risk, so some degree of risk-taking is inevitable, but we should only take appropriate risks in relation to the level of return we expect or require.
4 **Risk has two key dimensions** – uncertainty can be expressed as "probability" or "frequency", and how much it matters can be called "impact" or "consequence."
5 **Risk management requires an understanding of both dimensions** – if the uncertain event is very unlikely or it would have negligible effect, it requires less attention.

6 Risk management is affected by perception – answers to the questions "How uncertain is it?" and "How much does it matter?" are subjective.

7 Perception is affected by many factors – including conscious rational assessment, subconscious sources of bias, and affective inner emotions (the "triple strand" of influences).

8 Risk attitude is "a chosen response to uncertainty that matters, driven by perception" – individuals and groups adopt risk attitudes either subconsciously or consciously, within a spectrum ranging from risk-averse to risk-seeking.

9 Risk attitude can be managed consciously – emotionally literate individuals and groups respond instead of reacting, understanding which risk attitude best meets the specific needs of the situation, and adopting the appropriate risk attitude.

10 Managed risk attitudes support effective risk management by promoting appropriate risk-taking – by managing risk attitudes proactively, individuals and groups can maximise the effectiveness of the way they manage risk, allowing them to take the appropriate amount of risk compared to the reward they are seeking.

Following these principles will ensure that we take the right risks for the right reasons, and will help us to make good decisions and achieve our objectives in a risky environment.

UNDERSTANDING RISK ATTITUDE

Risk management is essential for business and project success, because it focuses on addressing uncertainties proactively in order to minimise threats, maximise opportunities, and optimise achievement of objectives. However, in practice risk management often fails to meet expectations, as demonstrated by repeated business and project failures. Foreseeable threats materialise into problems and crises, and achievable opportunities are missed leading to lost benefits. Clearly some essential ingredient is missing.

There is wide agreement that people are the most significant Critical Success Factor for effective management of risk. Risk management is undertaken by people, acting individually and in various groups, with a multitude of influences both explicit and covert. People adopt risk attitudes that affect every aspect of the risk process, even if they are unaware of it. Understanding and managing these attitudes would significantly increase risk management effectiveness – so what are they?

> Risk management often fails to meet expectations, as demonstrated by repeated business and project failures.

Our simple definition of "risk" is "uncertainty that matters", and it is only possible to define a risk in relation to something specific, usually an objective of some kind. A person's view of risk is also affected by their perception of such things as the likelihood of the risk occurring or the impact if it were to happen. Similarly "attitude" is "a chosen response to a given situation", and it too is related to a specific situation and affected by perception. Combining the two definitions of "risk" and "attitude" allows us to build a working definition of "risk attitude": **"a chosen response to uncertainty that matters, influenced by perception".**

Risk attitudes exist on a continuous spectrum, although we usually refer to just a few headline terms. These include risk-averse (uncomfortable with uncertainty), through risk-tolerant (no strong response), to risk-seeking (welcoming uncertainty), with a fourth risk attitude of risk-neutral (taking a long-term view). The risk attitude spectrum is illustrated in the figure below (except for risk-neutral), and each of the basic risk attitudes is also described in more details in the table. Risk attitudes are active at individual, group, corporate and national levels, and they need to be understood so that their influence on the risk process can be managed effectively.

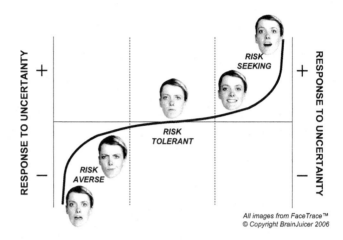

All images from FaceTrace™
© Copyright BrainJuicer 2006

It's relatively easy to describe these different risk attitudes, and then to work out which one is being displayed by a particular individual or group. But diagnosis is different from treatment. Sometimes the risk attitude initially adopted by an individual or group may not support effective management of risk, for example if a product innovation team is risk-averse, or if a nuclear safety inspector is risk-seeking. In these cases action may be required to modify risk attitude. Recent advances in the field of Emotional Intelligence and emotional literacy provide a means by which attitudinal change can be promoted and managed, for both individuals and organisations. The key is to recognise that all attitudes are a choice, and can therefore be modified.

This is a big subject, but the first step in applying emotional literacy to the management of risk attitude is self-awareness. This applies to both individual and groups. To start the process of understanding and managing risk attitude, four simple questions can be asked (replace "I/me/my" with "we/us/our" for a group):

1 How do I feel in this uncertain situation?
2 Why do I feel that?
3 Is my response appropriate to help me achieve my objectives?
4 If not, what am I going to do about it?

ATTITUDE	DEFINITION
Risk-averse	A conservative risk attitude with a preference for secure payoffs. Risk-averse individuals and groups are practical, accepting, and value common sense. They enjoy facts more than theories, and support established methods of working. They may feel uncomfortable with uncertainty, with a low tolerance for ambiguity, and be tempted to seek security and resolution in the face of risk. They may also tend to over-react to threats and under-react to opportunities.
Risk-seeking	A liberal risk attitude with a preference for speculative payoffs. People who are risk-seeking are adaptable and resourceful, enjoy life, and are not afraid to take action. They may underestimate threats, seeing them simply as a challenge to be overcome. They might also overestimate the importance of possible opportunities, wishing to pursue them aggressively.
Risk-tolerant	A balanced risk attitude with no strong reaction to uncertain situations. Risk-tolerant individuals and groups are reasonably comfortable with most uncertainty, accepting it as normal, and taking it in their stride with no apparent or significant influence on your behaviour. They may fail to appreciate the importance of threats and opportunities, tending to be reactive rather than proactive. This may lead to more problems from impacted threats, and loss of potential benefits as a result of missed opportunities.
Risk-neutral	An impartial risk attitude with a preference for future payoffs. People who are risk-neutral are neither risk-averse nor risk-seeking, but rather seek strategies and tactics that have high future payoffs. They think abstractly and creatively and envisage the possibilities. They enjoy ideas and are not afraid of change or the unknown. For both threats and opportunities they focus on the longer-term and only take action when it is likely to lead to significant benefit.

Academic researchers have studied risk psychology for many years, but there has not been much practical guidance on workplace application. Because risk attitude has such a major effect on all elements of the risk process, it is time to pay attention to this vital topic. Emotionally literate individuals and groups understand why they respond to risk in a particular way, and can adopt attitudes which are appropriate to the situation, helping them to maximise their risk management effectiveness.

WHAT DRIVES RISK ATTITUDES?

If we want to understand risk attitudes we need to be clear about the role of perception in shaping them. There are three major types of influence on the perception of risk, which we call the "triple strand." This is made up of conscious factors, subconscious factors, and affective factors. While the three parts of the triple strand overlap and interact in complex ways, it is helpful to tease out each of the three elements so that they can be examined and understood.

Conscious factors

These are the visible and measurable characteristics of a particular risky situation, based on our rational assessment. We also take account of situational factors such as whether we have done anything similar before (familiarity), the degree to which we have control of the situation (manageability), or how soon the situation is expected to affect us (proximity).

Subconscious factors

These include heuristics and other sources of cognitive bias. Heuristics are mental shortcuts based on our previous experience. Some heuristics help us to reach an appropriate position quickly, while others can be misleading. Unfortunately because heuristics are subconscious, their influence is often hidden, and they can be a significant source of bias. Common heuristics include memory of significant events (availability), or the conviction that we already know the right answer (confirmation trap).

Affective factors

These are gut-level visceral feelings and emotions which tend to rise up automatically or instinctively in a situation and influence how we react. Fear, excitement or attraction can lead us to adopt risk attitudes that a more rational assessment might not consider.

Conscious Factors
(situational assessments)

Subconscious Factors
(heuristics and cognitive bias)

Affective Factors
(feelings and emotions)

...together influence perception & risk attitude

The triple strand of influences interact together to form a complex web of factors that affect our perception in two important ways: how we perceive a particular risky situation, and our perception of the right way to respond to it. By appreciating how the triple strand factors drive our perception of risky situations, we will understand better why we adopt different risk attitudes. This will help us to manage our attitudes to risk proactively so that we make good decisions, select appropriate responses, and improve our management of risk.

IT'S JUST NOT RATIONAL

Dr Paul Slovic from Decision Research Inc (US) is a leading researcher in the field of risk psychology, and he has produced some valuable insights to help us understand how and why we feel the way we do towards risk. Although rational assessment is a significant contributor to how risky we believe a situation to be, there are also many non-rational factors that influence our perception of risk. Slovic lists the following:

1 Dread

If the outcome of a particular risk is something we imagine to be terrible, painful or fearful, our perception of the risk is heightened. For example, anything that might cause cancer is seen as a high risk because the thought of cancer evokes fear.

2 Control

Where we believe we have control, we perceive risk as lower. Travelling by car is a clear example – we feel less comfortable as a passenger than if we are driving.

3 Natural vs. man-made

Hazards resulting from human actions are seen as more risky than natural hazards. Nuclear power stations appear to pose greater risk than severe weather or natural disasters.

4 Choice

If I have some choice over my exposure to a risk, then it seems lower than if I am exposed involuntarily. For example, radiation from mobile-phone transmitters gets more public attention and action than exposure to solar radiation when sunbathing on holiday.

5 Children

Any risk that affects children is perceived as worse than one which only affects adults. Playground safety gets more attention than road safety.

6 Novelty

New risks are seen as being higher than ones we have grown used to seeing (genetically modified food is viewed as more risky than pesticides). And continued exposure to the same risk results in it being seen as less risky.

7 Publicity

If a risk has a high profile in the media or public consciousness, it will be perceived as being more risky. Terrorism is an obvious current example.

8 Propinquity

If I could be a victim, the importance of the risk seems higher than it really is. For example, I may worry about post-operative complications after surgery even if the hospital or surgeon have a good track record.

9 Risk-benefit trade-off

If exposure to a risk could also result in a perceived benefit as well as a threat, the risk is discounted. Key examples include smoking and drink-driving.

10 Trust

Where protection from a risk is offered from a trusted party, the risk is perceived as lower, but lack of trust makes the risk seem bigger. For example, public trust in government or the police can influence the perceived level of threat from terrorism or crime.

These non-rational factors have significant effects on how well risk is assessed and managed. Although Slovic's work relates to public perceptions of risk within society, his conclusions apply equally well to assessment of business and project risks. If we remain unaware of these factors, we are likely to make wrong judgements about how important a risk is, and our responses will be inappropriate. Recognising their existence can lead to more effective risk processes, more realistic risk communication, and better outcomes.

OPTIMIST, PESSIMIST ... OR REALIST?

The former British Prime Minister Winston Churchill once said: **"A pessimist sees the difficulty in every opportunity; an optimist sees the opportunity in every difficulty."** This exposes an interesting link between pessimism, optimism and risk attitude. One result of **pessimism** is an undue focus on threats that could lead someone to become risk-averse, wanting to avoid or minimise negative outcomes wherever possible, and becoming over-protective. On the other hand, **optimism** can produce an excessive concentration on opportunities, which can result in a risk-seeking attitude, looking for the upside in every uncertainty, and taking on too much risk exposure.

Always being either pessimistic or optimistic will not help us to be fully effective in managing risk. If we only look for threats we will miss potential benefits. But an exclusive focus on opportunities will result in problems happening that could have been avoided. Instead we need a proper balance between both perspectives, allowing trade-offs between threats and opportunities, in order to give us the best possible chance of achieving our goals. In place of pessimism or optimism, we need to aim for **realism**.

A realistic view of the situation will seek out both bad and good risks, including threats and opportunities. Both of these types of risk need to be identified and assessed so that we can develop and implement effective responses that will avoid or minimise threats while capturing or enhancing opportunities.

Always being either pessimistic or optimistic will not help us to be fully effective in managing risk.

The following steps will help us to ensure realism in our approach to managing risk:

- **Recognise and value different perspectives**

Our risk process should encourage and use input from both pessimists and optimists. We need to listen to people who warn us about what might go wrong, as they may have seen something that we have missed. We should also allow people to explore possible upsides that could result in unplanned gains.

- **Include peer challenge in the risk process**

The role of "devil's advocate" can be very useful in testing established attitudes to risk. Give someone the role of asking naïve or difficult questions during risk workshops: "Why do we always do it this way? Why can't we try something else? What if …?"

- **Use independent audits as a sense-check**

Bringing in an outsider to review the risk process and its outputs can reveal established or habitual tendencies to pessimism or optimism. An independent expert can suggest alternative ways of thinking or acting which might provide important new insights.

- **Monitor performance**

Comparing what actually happens with what was predicted can indicate whether we are being too negative or too hopeful. This can allow corrective action to be taken to adjust for sources of bias arising from either pessimism or optimism.

- **Manage risk attitudes**

Individuals and groups should learn to understand their risk attitudes and be able to modify them if necessary. Emotional literacy offers a range of helpful techniques that can be used to support proactive management of risk attitude, helping us to counter pessimism or optimism and choose the appropriate risk attitude that will support the achievement of our objectives.

It is easy to categorise ourselves or other people as pessimists or optimists, and allow ourselves to be forced into adopting inappropriate attitudes to risk. Instead we should recognise the bias that these mindsets can produce, and we should aim to be realistic in our assessment of the true risk exposure that we face. Only then will we be able to manage risks effectively.

MOTIVATE!

Although most people would agree that risk management is "A Good Thing", it is still widely practised with a lack of enthusiasm and commitment. If we want to motivate people and organisations to treat risk management more seriously, it might be worth considering established motivational theories. One of the best known of these is Abraham Maslow's "Hierarchy of Needs."

Maslow suggested that humans are motivated by the drive to satisfy a range of different needs, but not all needs are equal. He arranged needs into a pyramid in order of their strength of influence as motivators, as shown here:

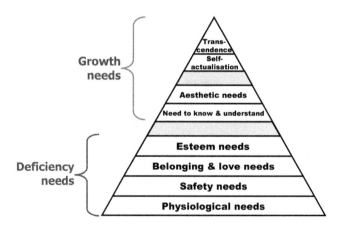

He believed that people are driven to satisfy lower needs before higher needs exert any influence. So for example, the most basic needs of air, water, sleep and food must be met first, and these are the over-riding concern of each individual, even more important than being safe or feeling self-esteem. Once these are satisfied a person is free to be concerned about other things. As each level of "hunger" is met (with literal physical hunger at the lowest level), higher needs emerge which require satisfying.

Maslow's hierarchy is divided into two groups, with "**deficiency needs**" towards the base, and "**growth needs**" at the top. Deficiency needs are mostly physical and emotional, and they must be satisfied or a person will feel anxious and incomplete. Growth needs by contrast are psychological and spiritual, and they are not essential for a healthy existence, but they make a person more fully rounded and complete.

How is this relevant to the challenge of motivating individuals and organisations to manage risk? The two levels of Maslow's hierarchy explain why risk management matters:

* **Deficiency needs** are about survival, which means responding to **threats**. In risk management terms, this is the realm of business continuity and disaster recovery, which aim to protect the business and ensure corporate survival, as well as operational risk management, health & safety, and a project risk process that addresses technical threats.

* By contrast, **opportunities** appear in Maslow's hierarchy as **growth needs**, since they are risks that, if they occurred, would have a positive effect. These exist in such areas as marketing and business development, as well as strategic decision-making, and they can also be found at project level in the form of project opportunities that help us to work faster, smarter or cheaper.

It is interesting that Maslow's Hierarchy of Needs predicts that where there are limited resources for risk management (which is most of the time), it is natural to address threats before opportunities, since threats operate at the lower levels of the hierarchy and lead to deficiency needs, whereas opportunities exist at the higher levels and are therefore seen as lower priority. However just as Maslow encourages us to address all needs at every level in the hierarchy if we are to become whole people, so the best approach to risk management is an integrated process which seeks both to minimise threats and maximise opportunities.

How can this understanding help us to motivate people to use risk management properly, not just in order to comply with procedures or standards, but as a positive contributor to project and business success? Maslow teaches us that needs exist and they must be satisfied, and that not all needs are equally important. Risk management must be seen to meet the needs of both individuals and organisations, providing real assistance as we respond to the challenges of our projects and business. We should recognise that dealing properly with risk will minimise our exposure to harmful threats, and fulfil our most basic needs for project and business survival.

The best approach to risk management is an integrated process which seeks both to minimise threats and maximise opportunities.

Maslow also emphasises the importance of an integrated approach addressing both deficiency needs (threats) and growth needs (opportunities). Including opportunities within our risk process will take us beyond mere survival into positive areas that create competitive advantage and sustainable growth.

We will only motivate people to take risk management seriously if we can demonstrate that it meets real needs, and Maslow points the way.

TOO BUSY? NO WAY!

What if people resist, complaining they're too busy to add risk management to their normal job? Well anyone who is too busy for risk management is too busy! People who have no time to think about potential problems in advance, always manage to make time to fix problems when they happen. A combination of the following eight steps should encourage them to adopt risk management:

1 Mandate it
If you can, it might help to insist that a structured risk management process must be implemented. While it is not the whole answer, it sometimes helps to tell people what to do. If your company procedures include a risk process, then you can refer to this and explain that there is really no choice.

2 Simplify it
Risk management need not be complicated. Make the process as simple as possible without compromising effectiveness. Minimise the overhead, keep risk meetings short and focused, and only collect information that you intend to use.

3 Normalise it
Explain that managing risk is a "normal task" for everyone, and it is not an optional extra. Every business or project is risky, and risk management needs to be built into every part of it. Plan and review risk responses the same as other tasks, and expect your team to treat them just like any other task.

4 Demonstrate it

Managers should lead by example, and be a role model for their team. If they show they are serious about identifying and managing risk, and actively do it themselves, the team are more likely to follow the example.

5 Use it

When risk reports are written and forgotten, people will learn that risk management is not important. But where the direction and strategy is adjusted in the light of risk information, they will see that their efforts make a difference to how the business or project is run.

6 Update it

If the Risk Register is produced once and never updated, or agreed responses are not reviewed and monitored, the risk assessment will quickly become outdated and useless. Ensuring that current risk exposure is understood emphasises the importance of the risk process.

7 Celebrate it

Look for proof that risk management has tackled a threat so that a problem was avoided, or evidence that a potential opportunity has been converted into a real advantage. Record these successes and tell people about them. Success breeds success.

8 "Pull" it

Seek the support and buy-in of senior management. When the boss asks for risk information as part of governance, people will know that it matters.

These steps should ensure people know how importantly the company views risk management, and should encourage them to take it seriously and do it themselves – because it works!

WHAT ABOUT INTUITION?

Human beings are a complex mixture of rational and irrational, a subtle combination of head, heart and guts. But when it comes to making decisions and managing risk, we seem to favour thinking over feeling. We believe that decision-making and risk management should be structured processes, dispassionately considering options, objectively weighing the odds, and reaching a result that can be fully justified and defended. Yet excluding the non-rational can deny us an important source of information, particularly when dealing with uncertainty. Is there a place for intuition in decision-making or risk management?

What is intuition? It describes "instinctive knowing without use of rational processes," a sense or feeling about something, that can't be easily explained or justified. Sometimes we "just know it seems right," or sometimes we consider "it feels wrong somehow." Should these feelings be dismissed automatically as unreliable and irrelevant, or is there some way we can use them?

> Excluding the non-rational can deny us an important source of information, particularly when dealing with uncertainty.

Intuition is often the result of extensive experience, the product of embedded wisdom, and the voice of distilled expertise. Someone who has worked in an area for a long time will probably have a deep understanding of the issues and complexities involved, and may form a judgement without being able to explain precisely how they got there. This rich source of experience should not be rejected lightly, but should be used to improve decision-making and risk management. But how?

Should we abandon all structured processes and instead just ask experts to tell us what they feel is right?

The right solution is not "either/or" but "both/and." We should combine intuition with a more rational approach, to get the best of both worlds. This involves the following three steps:

- **Listen**

Use intuition to validate the outputs of our decision-making and risk processes.

- **Learn**

Seek to capture the embedded knowledge of experts, and make it available for others to use.

- **Grow**

Develop our own intuitive skills through practice and feedback.

There is however a potential danger in using intuition as part of risk or decision-making processes. Because it is based on previous experience, intuition is highly specific to the individual, and it may therefore be biased and unrepresentative. It depends on the particular experience of each person. Consequently we need to be aware of the underlying basis for intuitive judgements.

We should aim to turn tacit or hidden knowledge into explicit or open knowledge wherever possible. This enables intuitive assessments to be validated, challenged where necessary, and used with confidence.

So there's nothing wrong with intuition, as long as it's used wisely. It can form a valuable part of the risk management process, helping us to find hidden risks and ensuring that our assessments and planned responses make sense. Intuition is also an important contributor to effective decision-making, tapping into reserves of previous experience and wisdom, and ensuring that the outcome is robust.

While it would be unwise to rely exclusively on intuition when making decisions or assessing risk, it would be equally imprudent to ignore this rich source of experience.

So risk management is a vital part of business, a process which, when effectively managed, will allow to us to work smarter, faster and cheaper and make the most of the experience, wisdom and expertise of our managers and staff. This chapter has shown how the people side of managing risk is at least as important as the process. But risk management also has invaluable application to the wider world, as we shall see in our next chapter.

5

The Wider World

Risk management practitioners can learn much from the wider world – and society has much to gain from learning lessons from the risk management process. This chapter takes a broader look at how the principles and practice of risk management are applied in some important areas beyond business, and asks what lessons we can learn.

AFTER THE CRISIS

Many people blame the global financial crisis on a failure of risk management. They say that risk professionals should have been in the best position to foresee what was coming and warn the rest of us. If the forward-looking radar of risk management was unable to spot the danger signs, then it can be of little use in future. Perhaps we should rely on something else to make sure that we don't make a similar mistake again.

Risk specialists tell a different story. They claim that they did indeed recognise the warning signs of overexposure in the financial markets and they raised these concerns within their organisations, but they were overruled by the business lines. It seems as if risk practitioners told their colleagues about the dangers and the decision was made to go ahead and take the risk anyway.

It is hard to judge at this point which of these versions of history are right, and perhaps the truth lies somewhere between the two. However attention is now turning to what should be done in the future. The following suggestions might prove useful as elements of a solution.

- **Avoid over-regulation.** There is an increasing call for much tighter
  regulation of the sectors that caused the problems. This may be a
  mistake for two reasons. Firstly, regulations are usually developed
  in response to a specific set of circumstances. In particular they are
  designed to prevent a recurrence of the current difficulties. However
  like generals who tend to use the strategies and tactics of the last
  war to fight the next one, such retrospective action is likely to be
  ineffective. Future challenges will be different from past ones, and
  they will need to be addressed using different approaches. Secondly,
  over-regulation can stifle creativity and innovation, and prevent us
  from developing the new ways of thinking and doing business that
  will be appropriate for the future. We need a level of regulation
  which is appropriate: not so restrictive that it will hold us back from
  the right level of risk-taking, but not so loose that it will allow the
  mistakes of the past to be repeated.

- **Recognise the role of risk management.** Senior management
  must view the contribution of their risk specialists as valuable
  input to both strategic and tactical decision-making. The risk
  management function must no longer be seen as the "Business
  Prevention Department", always raising objections and trying to
  stop people from making progress or profits. Instead the insights
  and recommendations that arise from the risk process should be
  welcomed, providing early warning of those uncertainties that matter,
  and allowing proactive action to be taken. This may mean raising the
  profile of risk management within the organisation, setting it on an
  equal footing with the business lines, with board-level representation
  and accountability.

- **Talk the same language.** Too often risk practitioners use their
  own jargon and fail to communicate their message clearly. Risk
  specialists need to express their findings and advice in language
  that will be understood by those who need to hear it. This means
  not talking about Risk Registers, Monte Carlo simulation or

Probability-Impact matrices. Instead they must present risk results in terms of what matters to the people who receive the information. Senior management are interested in strategy, business value and competitive advantage. Technical experts are more concerned with functionality and performance. Risk communication should not be an afterthought but should receive careful attention and planning.

- **Remember that risk includes opportunity.** Not all risk is bad, and aggressive attempts to reduce risk too far will prevent us from exploiting the upside and capturing the rewards that appropriate risk-taking offers. Seeking opportunities through the risk process can create competitive advantage, maximise value and provide innovative solutions. A proper emphasis on this positive side of the risk equation will bring significant benefits as we emerge from the global financial crisis and move forward into the new unknown.

We face an uncertain future and no-one can be sure what the post-crisis world will look like. We can however be sure that being successful will require an effective approach to dealing with uncertainty, and risk management will play an important part in that success.

RISK MANAGEMENT – AN UNAFFORDABLE LUXURY?

Are there any valid reasons for keeping risk management in straitened times when all non-essential costs are rightly being removed wherever possible? In the light of the serious economic situation and general downturn in business and the markets, organisations have required severe and radical cost reduction measures, using a range of euphemisms such as belt-tightening, efficiency savings, and re-engineering the cost base. All non-essential costs have been identified and cut in an attempt to reduce the pain felt by organisations large and small, in the hope of increasing their survivability in difficult times. And the list of so-called non-essentials has included all the usual victims: recruitment "on hold" or staff "let go", new investments in product development or R&D delayed or shelved, budgets for training and other forms of staff development reduced, and so on.

While these cost-cutting measures may be effective in the near term, they are of course short-sighted, since recruitment, research and staff skills are vital contributors to the ongoing health and performance of any organisation. It is only a matter of time before businesses have to return to these practices, since they represent necessary investments rather than avoidable costs.

There is one new entry on the list of potential cost savings, which some suggest is a natural candidate for removing unnecessary cost from any organisation, namely risk management. Several potential clients have told us they would like to establish or improve their approach to risk management, but they were being hampered by budgetary constraints.

The argument is that since risks are merely uncertain future events that may never happen, there is no need to spend time and effort (and therefore cost) on identifying, assessing and managing them. Instead the organisation should ensure that its fundamental structures and processes are sound and resilient, and should only react when it is absolutely necessary to do so, if risks materialise into actual events.
Reducing the effort spent on risk management produces cost savings in two ways. Firstly, staff are not spending time on the risk process, attending risk workshops, producing Risk Registers or reports, or reviewing risk assessments to keep them up to date. Secondly, time and money will not be spent on new actions that are deemed necessary to respond to identified risks. Cut risk management and you can remove the dual costs of assessing risks and of addressing risks, or so the argument goes.

As a risk specialist, you might expect the Risk Doctor to object to this approach, and you'd be right! There are indeed strong arguments against including risk management in cost-cutting measures. Firstly, risk management should be seen in the same light as many of the other so-called "non-essential costs", such as recruitment, research or training. Risk management is an investment in an organisation's ability to cope with an uncertain future. It is not a pure cost, since the goal of risk management is to provide sufficient advance warning of significant risks to allow threats to be avoided or minimised, and to exploit and maximise opportunities. Time and effort allocated to managing risk in advance should be seen as "spend to save" (by stopping potential bad things from happening so we don't have to deal with them later), or as "spend to gain" (by capturing additional benefits and creating value).

Secondly, a proper understanding of risk exposure will allow an organisation to set aside appropriate levels of contingency to cope with the effects of likely future uncertainties. Instead of hoping to muddle through and cope with any unexpected crisis "if and when it occurs" (as it surely will), targeted resources can be pre-positioned ready to be used when the need arises. This will contribute to the flexibility and resilience that are so vital to organisational survival in turbulent times.

Finally, for an organisation serious about cost reduction and efficiency savings, risk management offers analysis and actions that aim to reduce waste, cut rework, maximise productivity, and support successful delivery. Avoiding and minimising threats naturally cuts out additional costs, by proactively dealing with potential problems before they have a chance to have any negative effect. And a risk process that includes opportunity management will automatically result in performance that is faster, smarter and cheaper.

There is no doubt that all sectors of industry and society face real challenges in coping with the fallout from the global financial crisis. But risk management should not be regarded as a non-essential cost to be cut. Instead organisations should use the insights offered by the risk process to ensure that they can handle the inevitable uncertainties and emerge in the best possible position in future. In times of high levels of volatility, risk management is more needed than ever, and cutting it is a false economy. Rather than treating risk management as part of the problem, we should see it as a major part of the solution.

LEARNING FROM COUNTER-TERRORISM

Britain has had a long-term strategy for countering international terrorism since 2003, known as CONTEST. (Some consultants probably earned a huge fee for coming up with this name, which appears to reflect the struggle and fight against terrorism, while simply being a contraction of COuNter TErrorism STrategy!)

CONTEST has four strands, known as the Four Ps: Prevent, Pursue, Protect and Prepare. So what do they mean, how do they work and where does risk management come in? The first two Ps aim to reduce the overall threat to the British public from international terrorism, while the second two Ps seek to reduce the extent of our vulnerability. Each strand has a very specific goal, with a range of associated actions to put it into practice:

- **Prevent** terrorism by tackling its underlying causes, particularly trying to address the radicalisation of individuals in the UK and elsewhere, dealing with underlying structural problems such as inequalities and discrimination, and challenging the ideologies used to support terrorism.

- **Pursue** terrorists and those who sponsor them, disrupting terrorist planning and activities through intelligence and action, both at home and abroad, including international cooperation with allies and partners.

- **Protect** the public and UK interests in the UK and overseas, to reduce vulnerabilities to attack by strengthening border security, protecting key utilities and transport infrastructures, and paying special attention to crowded public places.

- **Prepare** for the consequences of a terrorist attack, by assessing possible impacts, building the necessary capabilities to respond to any attacks that might occur, regularly evaluating and testing preparedness, and learning lessons from exercises and real events.

With Government spending £2 billion annually on counter-terrorism, intelligence and resilience, with particular effort focused on the Prevent strand of CONTEST, citizens could be reassured that this threat is taken seriously, and that a structured and comprehensive approach has been developed and is being implemented.

How is the UK Government's counter-terrorism strategy relevant to business? Fortunately most of our concerns have nothing to do with terrorism or malicious threats to human life and security, although these are real issues that can't be neglected. We do however face many other types of threats that require our serious and structured attention. Can we learn anything from CONTEST and the Four Ps?

Threats, as we know, are uncertain future events or sets of circumstances that may never occur. However if they were to happen, they would have a negative effect on one or more of our objectives. This means threats have two key characteristics, which we have labelled as "probability" (how likely is it to happen?) and "impact" (what would the result be?). The main way we deal with threats in the context of business is through risk management, which offers a structured approach to identify, assess and respond to all types of risks (including both threats and opportunities).

The response development part of the risk process is where we try to find appropriate ways to tackle each identified risk, and some believe that this is the most important element of managing risk. After all, if our responses are ineffective then risk exposure remains unchanged, or we may even make it worse. On the other hand, effective risk responses will reduce risk exposure and give us the best chance of meeting our project objectives.

Response development is where the Four Ps come in. The first two Ps tackle the probability side of the threat equation. **Prevent** seeks to reduce the chance of a threat arising in the first place, by tackling its underlying causes. And **Pursue** aims to disrupt the processes that might lead a threat to turn into a real event, minimising the probability of a successful attack. The impact dimension of threat is addressed by the second two Ps. The **Protect** strand ensures that our vulnerability to a threat is as low as practicably possible, while **Prepare** provides contingency plans to deal quickly and effectively with any events that might actually happen.

Those responsible for addressing risk in business could learn a lot from considering these Four Ps of counter-terrorism. They offer different insights into ways of tackling the threats we face every day in our projects and organisations, and could help us to find more effective responses. Hopefully we won't directly encounter the menace of terrorism, but we should be as determined as the Government to take all necessary steps to deal with the threats we do face.

NIGHTMARE ON DOWNING STREET

When the UK Government published its first National Risk Register in 2008, detailing the most significant risks facing the nation as a whole, it aroused a lot of media interest and comment as people were confronted with what keeps ministers awake at night, as well as details of what they are doing about it.

The UK National Risk Register presents twelve risks which are assessed as having the potential to have a major impact on the country: pandemic influenza, coastal flooding, major industrial accidents, attacks on critical infrastructure, inland flooding, attacks on crowded places, major transport accidents, non-conventional attacks, attacks on transport, severe weather, animal disease and electronic attacks.

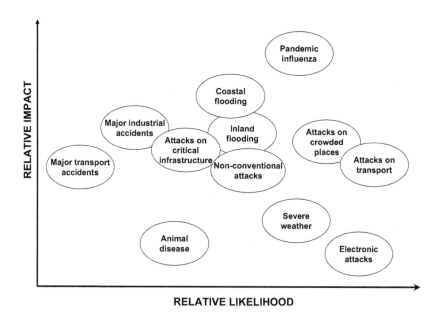

Of course these are not the only risks faced by the UK, but they were selected as representing the biggest risks currently requiring attention and action, since occurrence of any one of these risks would result in a national emergency. The scales of likelihood and impact are also relative not absolute, so being close to the lower left-hand corner does not mean "low likelihood/low impact", just that that risks in this position are assessed as being less likely or with less impact than the others.

While the UK National Risk Register covers national emergencies that might occur in the coming five-year timeframe, and is limited to accidents, natural events and malicious attacks, there is much that we can learn about how to assess the risks that might affect business.

First the UK National Risk Register has a very **clear scope**. It only covers risks that would result in an emergency as defined by the Civil Contingencies Act 2004. All risk assessments must also have a properly defined scope, stating what is "at risk", so that risks can be identified that are relevant.

The likelihood and impact of the risks in the UK National Risk Register were assessed against **clear criteria**. Likelihood was based on historical data where possible, otherwise the judgement of experts was used. Impact was measured against five dimensions, including human illness or injury, fatalities, social disruption, economic damage, and the psychological impact on society. Companies should also assess likelihood using previous information when that is available, and expert judgement when it is not. And the impacts of risks should be assessed in multiple dimensions, not just money, reflecting various objectives (such as timeline, performance, delivered value, quality etc).

The **timeline** for the UK National Risk Register is defined as the coming five years, and each risk is assessed in relation to that period. Business risk assessments are often confused over whether the risk is being assessed as a single occurrence or over a defined period such as the lifetime of a project, or a strategic planning cycle.

The purpose of the UK National Risk Register is clearly stated as being to prioritise the most important risks so that **appropriate action** can be taken, and it presents details of what the UK Government and emergency services are doing in relation to each risk. In the same way, the risk process in business must not stop with identifying and assessing risks. Risk management is not complete until risks are managed. That means deciding on what to do, and turning plans into actions.

The UK National Risk Register is seen as the highest-level document describing risks to the nation, but it feeds into lower-level Community Risk Registers that consider risks and their impacts at a more local level. Organisations should also use Risk Registers at **different levels**, including project, programme, business and strategic, and these must be aligned to allow risks to be escalated and delegated between levels, so that they can be managed at the most appropriate place in the organisation.

The UK has been described as a pioneer in coordinated risk management for emergencies because of the systematic way in which we assess the risks and use these assessments to help planning.

When the UK National Risk Register was first published, there was a lot of discussion in the media over what was "the top risk faced by the UK". The UK National Risk Register is quite careful not to list the risks in priority order, and says they are all important and need to be managed. However it was interesting to see how the media interpreted the diagram on page 182. Most reports picked out "pandemic influenza" as the top risk, presumably because it has the highest relative impact, even though there are other risks that are assessed as being more likely.

This arises from a natural tendency to treat impact as more important than likelihood, which in extreme cases results in an over-protective and inappropriately risk-averse approach being taken towards risks. Companies should be careful to define their risk prioritisation method clearly in advance, so that everyone knows the thresholds against which risks are assessed, and everyone can be clear about which really are the top risks.

The UK National Risk Register opens with a claim from the UK Government that, "The UK has been described [by the World Economic Forum (WEF)] as one of the pioneers in coordinated risk management for emergencies because of the systematic way in which we assess the risks and use these assessments to help planning." It closes by saying that, "Publication of this National Risk Register will mean that the UK will meet most of the principles of country risk management established by the WEF."

This raises a vital question for business: are we producing our Risk Registers just so that we meet the requirement and tick the right boxes? Or are we using risk information to help us plan and execute our requirements in the best possible way?

We should congratulate the UK Government for publishing the first UK National Risk Register and taking seriously the major risks faced by our country. We should also follow their example when managing risks in business, so that our Risk Registers are also recognised and used as valuable contributors to success.

MAN OVERBOARD!

Sailing is becoming increasingly popular in the UK, both for pleasure and as a serious sport. More young people are also taking up sailing, and the Royal National Lifeboat Institution (RNLI) has run a special education campaign to encourage young people to be safe at sea. The SAFE campaign has four simple elements:

- Spot the dangers.
- Always go with a friend.
- Find and read the safety signs.
- Emergency? Stick up your hand and shout.

This simple set of messages contains all the important advice needed to stay safe at sea, and has probably saved lives.

Source: © istockphoto/Sergey Ivanov

The SAFE campaign can also save a lot of trouble if we translate its four elements into the business environment.

The first step is to **"Spot the dangers."** The best time to do this is before you set sail, but it's also vital to stay alert while at sea as conditions can change quickly and new dangers can arise unexpectedly. In business, the risk management process is designed to spot the dangers in advance, giving an organisation early warning of what might happen.

When we see potential dangers in advance, we can plan how to respond in order to minimise our exposure. We can set a course that avoids the major risks and try to minimise the risks we can't remove. And like staying safe at sea, we need to monitor the risk situation constantly, staying alert for emergent risks and changing course where necessary. So the first step to following the RNLI SAFE code in business is to give proper attention to the risk management process.

Two pairs of eyes have a better chance of seeing potential dangers than one, and two pairs of hands can deal with most situations.

The second piece of advice from RNLI to young sailors is, **"Always go with a friend."** There's nothing worse than getting into trouble on your own. Two pairs of eyes have a better chance of seeing potential dangers than one, and two pairs of hands can deal with most situations. Most of the time business is also not a single-handed sport, and managers and their teams have a vital role in keeping it on track and dealing with things that arise unexpectedly. The risk process should take input from a range of stakeholders to ensure that as many risks as possible are identified and managed effectively.

The manager who tries to go it alone may emerge as a solitary hero, but is more likely to miss something important and get into trouble. In contrast the manager who involves his colleagues or the team will have a wider range of experience and expertise to draw on when it comes to managing risks. In addition it will be helpful for a manager to have an older and wiser colleague who they can ask for advice when they get into new situations outside their previous experience. Managers should always take a friend with them when they are managing an important or risky endeavour.

Refusing to ask for help when things go badly wrong is a sign of weakness not strength.

The third RNLI SAFE element is to "**Find and read the safety signs**." These include both permanent signs that indicate dangers often encountered by sailors at this location, as well as temporary signs put up to warn of specific situations that are currently occurring. Companies can find similar "safety signs" in several places. Firstly they should learn from the previous experience of others who have done similar sorts of work before them, to avoid making the same mistakes again. The lessons learned knowledge base should contain a range of warnings about problems, issues and risks previously encountered, together with suggestions for dealing with these.

In addition the routine management processes developed by the organisation provide tried and tested ways of addressing common challenges and risks. These standard operating procedures should exist for a reason, and managers must know them and follow them. Ignoring these "safety signs" exposes the business to additional risks, but taking time to become familiar with them will be a worthwhile investment and could save the project from a lot of unnecessary trouble.

The final piece of advice to stay SAFE at sea is an essential last resort. **"Emergency? Stick up your hand and shout!"** When all else fails and you actually get into trouble, don't struggle and sink in silence. Make some noise, attract some attention, get some help! Too many managers seem reluctant to admit when they get into difficulties. Perhaps it is part of an organisational culture that only rewards success, or maybe it comes from an attitude that managers must be "can-do heroes".

But refusing to ask for help when things go badly wrong is a sign of weakness not strength. We need to know where to look for assistance, perhaps with a couple of more experienced mentors or advisors on hand. And we need to make some noise if our business or project is in danger of sinking without trace, so that we can be rescued and live to sail again. Getting help fast will prevent disaster and ensure survival.

So we should thank RNLI for providing some sound risk management advice. The SAFE campaign has made sure that more young people stay safe while sailing at sea, and allowed them to enjoy this great sport without coming to harm. Following the same four SAFE principles can also save your business or project from sinking without trace, and ensure that you make it safely to your intended harbour.

LET'S GET PERSONAL

We can apply risk management to a broad range of activities, wherever we can define distinct objectives. This includes **personal risk management**, identifying and managing uncertainties that could affect achievement of our personal objectives.

As with any other application area, personal risk management can be applied at different levels of detail. The key lies in how well we are able to **specify our personal objectives**. At the highest level we might say that our aim is to be "happy, healthy, wealthy and wise" or perhaps to "live long and prosper", and we can identify and manage strategic personal risks which might affect these broad goals. This might require us to address big issues such as our key personal relationships, diet and exercise regime, or investment and pension policies.

Or we might identify more specific personal objectives such as, "Reduce my weight by 20 pounds by the end of June", or "Learn to speak a foreign language fluently before my summer holidays", or "Obtain promotion within 12 months." For each of these specific objectives we can then apply the risk management process to help us reach them.

The process is exactly the same as any other application of risk management. After **defining objectives**, the next step is to **identify risks**, including both threats that could hinder us as well as opportunities that could help us. For a career development objective for example, downside risks might include the following: I might be assigned to a new job which absorbs all my time and energy; I might invest in training which does not provide the required new skills or knowledge; I might set unrealistic expectations and give up. On the upside, a new opening may arise at work or elsewhere; I might be able to use completely different skills to move into a new area; I might meet someone who offers me my ideal next job.

After risk identification comes **assessment**, estimating the probability and impact of each identified risk to prioritise them for further action. Simple "high/medium/low" scales can be used for this, enabling the worst threats and best opportunities to be found.

This needs to be followed by **response development**, finding appropriate and effective actions to minimise threats and maximise opportunities. Some of these might be simple (talk to my boss or colleagues about possible internal openings; research available training courses), and others may require more effort and investment (obtain coaching to explore my deep-seated personal goals; join professional association to improve networking).

Finally, identified responses need to be **implemented**, and their effect should be **monitored**, to see whether they are moving us towards our objective. Where necessary, we should develop new responses, remaining alert to the possibility of secondary risks. And our risk assessment should be **updated** regularly to find and respond to new threats and opportunities.

Personal risk management involves reviewing where we are currently in relation to where we want to be, and developing strategies and actions to change where necessary. Risk management is not just for work or business – it can help us achieve our personal objectives as well. Try applying the risk process to your personal life and see what a difference it can make!

DANGER AHEAD

What does the future hold? When I was growing up, we were looking forward to the leisure society when robots would do all the household chores and repetitive work tasks, and the biggest problem would be deciding how to fill the work-free days. Space travel would be commonplace and we could choose to live under the sea or on the moon as viable alternatives to the land. Wearable computers would be controlled by our thoughts, all diseases would have been eradicated, and driverless cars would travel on congestion-free roads or skyways powered by cheap energy from cold-fusion reactors. Of course we were also scared by the prospect of World War III and a nuclear holocaust, but on balance the future looked positive and exciting. What happened?!

Danish physicist Niels Bohr reminded us that, "Prediction is always difficult, especially about the future", yet it is the purpose of risk management to act as a forward-looking radar to scan the uncertain future and help us prepare for it. But what is it about the future that makes it so uncertain? Perhaps we should just expect continuity with more of the same?

Expecting the immediate future to be a continuation from the immediate past is a dangerous mistake. The following six characteristics of the future explain why there might be DANGER ahead.

1 Dynamic
The future is changing. Even if we think that right now we have a reasonably good view of what might happen in the future, by the time the future actually arrives it will have changed significantly. The future we see today is constantly changing and it will be different when we look at it tomorrow or next week.

2 Ambiguous
We do not have sufficient information today to enable us to understand or interpret the future fully. There are aspects of the future that are not yet clear, and we must recognise the limitations of our ability to make sense of it from our current perspective.

3 Non-linear
It is not possible to draw a straight line from the past to the future. We cannot work out what might happen by analysing the past and simply

extending it forward. Such extrapolation is based on the assumption that the past is a good predictor of the future. While that may have been the case previously, it may not always continue to be true. Just because the past past was a good indicator of the past future doesn't mean that the future past will be a good indicator of the future future!

4 "Glocal"

Developments in the future are likely to be a combination of global and local. We have become used to globalisation as a fact of life, and also to the need for action at the level of local communities. This polarisation may collapse with a new emphasis on "think global – act local", the use of technology to eliminate the significance of geographical distance, and the empowering of local communities to exercise wider influence beyond their natural horizons.

5 Emergent

New forces and factors will arise in the future that are not currently visible or imaginable. These are currently "unknown unknowns" (sometimes called Black Swans), as we have already seen. We can try to improve our predictive capability, but there will always be surprises, both good and bad.

6 Relational

The future will be more dependent on people and the relationships between them, with technology playing an enabling and supportive role. This will be increasingly important at all levels, including family, community, society and national. We must understand how people function as individuals and how they interact in various groups, and we need to include the implications of these relationships in our models of the future.

If we want to use risk management as an effective forward-looking radar, to give us timely insights into what might be ahead, we need to fine-tune it to address these six characteristics of the future. We should be alert to their existence and to their likely influence on our projects, businesses and lives. And we should consider now how we might respond to these important factors in order to prepare ourselves for when the future becomes the present.

The future may hold DANGER, but risk management can help.

CHANGING THE FUTURE

Risk management scans the uncertain future ahead of us, trying to pick out the main features, both good and bad. The aim is to give us as much time as possible to decide what to do, with enough time to actually do it. Then we can steer away from things that might harm us (threats), and aim towards things that might help us (opportunities). This applies to our personal lives, our business prospects … and could provide valuable guidance for our political leaders, too.

As we examine our risk radar screen and try to discern the various alternative futures, we can classify them into three groups.

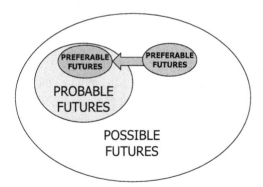

1 Possible Futures
Our first task is to decide whether a particular future scenario is possible or not. Of course we could imagine futures that are not theoretically

or physically possible, but these should be discarded quickly, without wasting time on analysing them. But even after removing the impossible ones, there will be a very large number of Possible Futures.

2 Probable Futures
These form a subset of Possible Futures, because they are not just possible, but they are more likely to happen than not. While we might not know precisely how probable a particular future really is, we can make an estimate, using both subjective and objective methods. Then we should concentrate our attention on the futures we think are most probable.

> The role of risk management is to ensure that Preferable Futures are Possible, then move them into the Probable zone.

3 Preferable Futures
Perhaps the most important futures of all are the ones we decide are preferable, the ones we really want to happen. Of course these should also be part of the Possible Futures set, but they may not be among the Probable Futures subset, at least initially.

How does this "futures analysis" relate to managing risk? The role of risk management is to ensure that Preferable Futures are Possible, then move them into the Probable zone. The following four steps explain how this can be achieved:

1 Understand the scope of Possible Futures
Standard strategic planning techniques can help here, including scenario analysis, futures thinking, Field Anomaly Relaxation, visualisation,

trend-watching, or environmental scans. This step demands creativity and innovation, to imagine a wide a range of possibilities.

2 Identify and assess the subset of Probable Futures

This is the realm of traditional risk assessment, considering the various Possible Futures and estimating how likely each one is to occur, and the outcome if it did actually happen.

3 Determine our desired Preferable Future

This step requires us to clearly define our objectives. These describe what we would like to see actually happening and what we intend to turn into reality. Often we have one most preferred future, although there may be a range of alternatives which are all good.

4 Manage the future

In the final step we take proactive decisions and actions in the present in order to affect the future. By identifying the drivers in each situation, we aim to maximise the chance of our Preferable Future actually happening, while trying to minimise the chances of occurrence of other Probable Futures that are undesirable.

People often think that they cannot affect the future, and the present is all that can be changed. Risk management takes a different view. Our decisions and actions in the present can influence the future. We can turn some Possible Futures into impossibilities, we can make some Probable Futures less likely, and we can turn our Preferable Future into reality. **Manage risk and change the future!**

THE LONGER VIEW FORWARD

We began this book with a **long view back**, charting the role of risk management from cave dwellers to the 21st century. Now it is time to look into our crystal ball and take the **longer view forward**.

Surveying the risk management futurescape, there are three possibilities for how risk management might develop. Drawing parallels from cosmology, we might call these three options "Infinite Expansion", "the Big Crunch", or "Ongoing Oscillation".

The expanding risk universe?

The first option is that the scope of risk management will continue to expand and include more and more elements of personal, business and social life, until "Everything is just risk management." Ultimately all decisions will be taken in the light of the identification and assessment of relevant uncertainty. This expansionist view is exemplified by some risk management practitioners whose slogan is, "Manage the risk = manage the business."

This implies that normal planned activity needs no special attention, and all that is required is management of variations from the plan. By looking ahead to identify potential variations, both positive and negative, and focusing management attention on addressing just these aspects, proponents of this position claim that success is ensured.

While the "Infinite Expansion" option emphasises the importance of risk management, it is an extreme position that doesn't match reality. The risk element is not the whole picture in a business or project, and concentrating wholly on managing risk to the exclusion of other aspects would be detrimental and counter-productive.

Catastrophe ahead?

It is probably true that the scope and influence of risk management will continue to expand, at least in the short term, as more areas of application are found for risk-based approaches. But is such expansion limitless, or will some critical point be reached when further growth is unsustainable, to be followed by a collapse and eventual "Big Crunch"?

It is possible that risk management might just be the latest management fad, although admittedly it is already rather more long-lasting than most. The recent emphasis on risk management started in the 1970s, and though it shows little sign of reducing, it is conceivable that our future colleagues might place less emphasis on risk than we do today. If risk management goes the way of other fads, it could disappear from the scene very quickly, becoming just a memory or a footnote in the annals of management history.

There is another way in which risk management might disappear, rather than fading away into oblivion. If risk management becomes all pervasive to the point where it is absorbed into the nature of business at all levels, it could become invisible as a result. If everyone naturally and habitually "thinks risk" and manages it as a normal part of daily life, then it might no longer be necessary to have a separate discipline called "risk management", since this would be accepted and practised by all. Risk management could vanish as a result of its own success, leaving risk specialists and practitioners as outdated purveyors of a universally recognised self-evident truth.

Constant change?

A third option for the future of risk management is possible, combining expansionism and catastrophism into "Ongoing Oscillation". Maybe the size of the "risk management universe" might vary cyclically, increasing for a time then contracting. A review of the broader story of risk management across the span of human history reveals periods when it was more prominent than others.

Social commentators suggest that advances in technology, law and religion can be seen as human responses to uncertainty, seeking to make sense of the ineffable, and attempting to impose control wherever possible. If this is true then the major changes in civilisations might be interpreted as cycles of risk management, though not within the same process-driven framework we see in modern business. And maybe the expansion we are witnessing today is merely part of the latest cycle.

Where now?

Only time will tell whether we'll see "Infinite Expansion" with the risk management universe expanding indefinitely until it encompasses everything, or whether a turning point might be reached to be followed by collapse to a "Big Crunch" where risk management disappears, or whether some "Ongoing Oscillation" cycle of growth and decline might occur. What is certain is that, like our physical universe, risk management is not in steady-state.

The reason that risk management is such a fascinating topic is precisely because it is constantly changing. New approaches and application areas emerge, new dimensions of risk management are discovered, and new insights into the meaning of risk are revealed. Explorers of this intriguing universe can be sure of an exciting journey as the future of risk management unfolds before them in novel and unexpected ways, challenging them "to boldly go where no man has gone before."

Changing the future doesn't need superpowers, just practical application of some of the lessons about risk management you have learned in this book. We conclude with a look at four simple steps you can take to make a difference.

Conclusion

Over to you

RISKY RESOLUTIONS

Now you have reached the end of this book, it's time to make four resolutions. If you stick to them, they can truly transform your life, projects and business.

Resolution 1: Be more risk-aware

The world is full of uncertainty, and there are a huge number of threats facing us at every turn, in our personal lives as well as professionally in our projects and business. We might adopt the "ostrich approach" to risk management, sticking our head in the sand and hoping that risk goes away. Of course this doesn't protect us at all, but it just might help us to stay more relaxed in the presence of risk – until it happens! It would be much better to face the fact that risk is everywhere, and adopt a more proactive approach towards it. Why not resolve to be more **risk-aware?**

Risk-awareness isn't a technique; it's a state of mind, being alert to risk all the time, seeking out possible uncertain events that could affect achievement of our objectives. And we mustn't forget to look for opportunities! A lot of the uncertainty that surrounds us could be helpful if only we recognised it in time. Sometimes embracing risk can create additional value, or allow an innovative approach that saves time and money. Proper risk-awareness needs to be double-sided, seeking out both upside and downside risks.

The "ostrich approach" to risk doesn't protect us, but it might help us to stay more relaxed – until the risk happens!

Resolution 2: Get integrated

If they do it at all, too many people do risk management in isolation, often as a bolt-on extra. Usually that's because we're busy doing "real work," and can't spare the time to think about things that might never happen. Risk management becomes a dispensable luxury, something to do "when I get a round tuit" – and since most people don't own a tuit of any shape, their risks don't get managed. And unmanaged risks lead to avoidable problems and reduced benefits. Instead of viewing risk management as an optional extra, you could resolve to **integrate** it into your normal activities.

Integrating risk management simply means treating it as "real work", and making sure that it fits with the rest of what you are doing. For example, when working on a project, think about risk when you make your initial estimates or draw up the project plan and resource profile. Use risk assessment as part of your change control process. Review risks at the regular management review meeting, and include a short risk section in all management reports. Used properly, risk management can inform and improve all aspects of the management of projects and business. Make your risk management "built-in not bolt-on" in order to get the full benefit.

> Risk management becomes something to do "when I get a round tuit"

Resolution 3: Take sensible risks

It's neither possible nor desirable to live life without taking risks. If we try to be safe all the time, and not expose ourselves to any uncertainty, we would never do anything. Projects in particular are risky by nature, and there is no such thing as a "zero-risk project". Of course we should try to reduce our risk exposure to a level that is acceptable, while not stifling creativity and innovation, but that level is not zero. That means we need to take some risk, and we shouldn't be afraid to admit it. But we should only take the level of risk that is consistent with our objectives and the level of return on offer. That means not acting irresponsibly or without proper consideration. Perhaps you should resolve to take more risks, but to do so sensibly?

Sensible risk-taking means identifying genuine risks, assessing them realistically, and acting appropriately. We should implement proactive responses where these are possible and cost-effective, and accept the residual risks. It means not being paralysed if there is any risk anywhere, but taking risk with our eyes open.

Resolution 4: Don't give up

The risk challenge is never-ending, and risk doesn't go away just because you've held one risk workshop and issued a Risk Register. Risk exposure is dynamic and changes frequently. That's why the risk process is iterative, repeating the cycle of risk identification, assessment, response planning, implementation and review on a regular basis. But sometimes we lose interest and get bored with doing the same things over again. We're fed up with having to update the Risk Register and think of new risks. We'd rather "file and forget." But this is bound to lead to problems – as risk is constantly changing, so our response to it must also stay up to date.

We can't do risk management once and think we've finished. We need to resolve to **keep going**; managing risk is a marathon not a sprint. A good way to help people persist with risk management is to reduce the administrative and bureaucratic burden as far as possible, making it easy to identify and manage risk. Then we should consider refreshing the risk process, perhaps trying new techniques, revising our report formats, or investing in some training. As the risk challenge evolves, so our approach to tackling it needs to be kept up to date.

There will be many threats and opportunities coming our way, which we need to deal with properly. So why not make these four resolutions, to make your risk management as effective as possible? And if you have trouble remembering these risky resolutions, it might help to think of them like this:

Risk-aware

Integrated approach

Sensible risk-taking

Keep going

Now it's over to you...

Epilogue

I hope this book has inspired you to take a fresh look at how you manage risk. With a few simple principles and a straightforward process it's easy to be prepared for the future, despite its inevitable uncertainties. The advice in these pages should help you to create value from risk, turning uncertainty to your advantage.

There is of course help available if you need it! Risk Doctor & Partners offers a range of specialist risk services which embody the approach outlined in this book. We have a team of expert risk practitioners around the globe who are able to tailor solutions to your specific requirements. We blend leading-edge thinking with practical application, providing access to the latest developments in risk management best practice. Our professional risk services include:

- **Coaching and mentoring**, providing personal input and support to key individuals or small teams, aiming to share and transfer expertise.

- **Organisational benchmarking**, using proven maturity models to understand current risk management capability in terms of risk culture, processes, experience and application, then defining realistic and achievable improvement targets and action plans to enhance capability.

- **Process review**, comparing your risk management approach against best practice and recommending practical improvements to meet the specific challenges faced by your business.

- **Risk review**, assessing the risk exposure of your project, programme or business, identifying and prioritising threats and opportunities, and developing effective responses to optimise performance and achievement of objectives.

*   **Risk training**, offering a range of learning experiences designed to raise awareness, create understanding and develop skills, targeting senior management, programme/project managers, project teams and risk practitioners.

There are many useful resources freely available from the Risk Doctor website (www.risk-doctor.com), including articles and papers for download, and an 'Ask the Doctor' service to raise specific queries.

Risk Doctor & Partners also maintains a network of people interested in risk management who want to keep in touch with latest thinking and practice. Network members receive regular email briefings from David Hillson on current issues in risk management. Click the "Join the RD Network" button from the Risk Doctor website.

Risk is everywhere and presents a range of threats and opportunities which need to be managed proactively if we are to minimise problems and maximise benefits. Risk Doctor & Partners offers high-value solutions for effective risk management. Get in touch to find out how you can benefit.

About the Author

Dr David Hillson CMgr FRSA FIRM FCMI HonFAPM is **The Risk Doctor**.
He is an international risk management consultant, and Director of Risk
Doctor & Partners (www.risk-doctor.com). He is recognised globally as
a leading thinker and expert practitioner in risk management, and he has
made several innovative contributions to the field. He consults, writes
and speaks widely on the topic and has received several awards for his
work. David's consulting, speaking and writing is shaped by his motto,
"Understand profoundly so you can explain simply", which ensures that
his work represents both sound thinking and practical application.

David has over 25 years experience in risk consulting and he has worked
in more than 40 countries, providing support to clients in every major
industry sector. David's input includes strategic direction to organisations
facing major risk challenges, as well as tactical advice on achieving
value and competitive advantage from effectively managing risk.

David is active in the Project Management Institute (PMI®) and received
the PMI Distinguished Contribution Award for his work in developing
risk management. He is also an Honorary Fellow of the UK Association
for Project Management (APM), where he has contributed to the risk
discipline over many years.

David is an active Fellow of the Institute of Risk Management (IRM),
and he was elected a Fellow of the RSA to contribute to its Risk
Commission. He is also a Chartered Manager and Fellow of the
Chartered Management Institute (CMI).

Useful References

RISK DOCTOR BOOKS

Hillson D. A. 2004. "Effective Opportunity Management for Projects: Exploiting positive risk." Boca Raton, USA: Taylor & Francis. ISBN 0-8247-4808-5

Hillson D. A. (ed) 2005. "Risky Rhymes: Uncertain wit & wisdom" Petersfield, UK: Risk Doctor Publishing. ISBN 0-9551338-0-7

Hillson D. A. (ed) 2007. "The Risk Management Universe: A guided tour" (revised edition). London, UK: British Standards Institution. ISBN 0-580-43777-9

Hillson D. A. & Simon P. W. 2007. "Practical Project Risk Management: The ATOM Methodology." Vienna VA, USA: Management Concepts. ISBN 978-1-56726-202-5

Hillson D. A. & Murray-Webster R. 2007. "Understanding and Managing Risk Attitude" (second edition). Aldershot, UK: Gower. ISBN 978-0-566-08798-1

Murray-Webster R. & Hillson D. A. 2008. "Managing Group Risk Attitude". Aldershot, UK: Gower. ISBN 0-566-08787-1

Hillson D. A. 2009. "Managing Risk in Projects" (part of Fundamentals of Project Management series, ed Dalcher D.). Farnham, UK: Gower. ISBN 978-0-566-08867-4

OTHER BOOKS

Apgar D. 2006. "Risk Intelligence: Learning to manage what we don't know". Boston MA, USA: Harvard Business School Press. ISBN 978-1-59139-954-4

Bernstein P. L. 1996. "Against the Gods – The remarkable story of risk". New York, USA: J Wiley. ISBN 0-471-12104-5

Chapman C. B. & Ward S. C. 2002. "Managing Project Risk and Uncertainty". Chichester, UK: J Wiley. ISBN 0-470-847905

Chapman R. J. 2006. "Simple Tools And Techniques for Enterprise Risk Management". Chichester, UK: J Wiley. ISBN 0-470-01466-0

Cleary S. & Malleret T. 2007. "Global Risk: Business success in turbulent times". Basingstoke, UK: Palgrave Macmillan. ISBN 978-0-230-52531-3

Cohen R. 2007. "The Second Bounce of the Ball: Turning risk into opportunity". London, UK: Wiedenfeld & Nicolson. ISBN 978-0-297-85147-9

Cooper D. F., Grey S., Raymond G. & Walker P. 2004. "Project Risk Management Guidelines: Managing risk in large projects and complex procurements". Chichester, UK: J Wiley. ISBN 0-470-02281-7

Flyvbjerg B., Bruzelius N. & Rothengatter W. 2003. "Megaprojects and Risk: An anatomy of ambition". Cambridge, UK: Cambridge University Press. ISBN 0-521-00946-4

Gardner D. 2008. "Risk: The science and politics of fear". London, UK: Virgin Books. ISBN 978-1-905264-15-5

Hulett D. T. 2009. "Practical Schedule Risk Analysis". Farnham, UK: Gower. ISBN 978-0-566-08790-5

Taleb N. N. 2007. "The Black Swan: The impact of the highly improbable". London, UK: Allen Lane/Penguin. ISBN 978-0-713-99995-2

Vose D. 2008. "Risk Analysis – A quantitative guide" (third edition). Chichester, UK: J Wiley. ISBN 978-0-470-51284-5

STANDARDS AND GUIDELINES

Association for Project Management. 2004 "Project Risk Analysis & Management (PRAM) Guide" (second edition). High Wycombe, UK: APM Publishing. ISBN 1-903494-12-5

Association for Project Management. 2008. "Prioritising Project Risks". High Wycombe, UK: APM Publishing. ISBN 978-1-903494-27-1

British Standard BS31100:2008 "Risk Management – Code of practice". London, UK: British Standards Institute. ISBN 978-0-580-57434-4

Institute of Risk Management (IRM), National Forum for Risk Management in the Public Sector (ALARM), & Association of Insurance and Risk Managers (AIRMIC). 2002. "A Risk Management Standard". London, UK: IRM/ALARM/AIRMIC.

Institution of Civil Engineers, Faculty of Actuaries and Institute of Actuaries. 2005. "Risk Analysis & Management for Projects (RAMP)" (second edition). London, UK: Thomas Telford. ISBN 0-7277-3390-7

International Organization for Standardization ISO31000:2009. "Risk Management – Principles and guidelines on implementation". Geneva, Switzerland: International Organization for Standardization.

Project Management Institute. 2008. "A Guide to the Project Management Body of Knowledge (PMBoK®)", Fourth Edition. Newtown Square PA, USA: Project Management Institute.

Project Management Institute. 2009. "The Practice Standard for Project Risk Management". Newtown Square PA, USA: Project Management Institute.

UK Office of Government Commerce (OGC). 2007. "Management of Risk: Guidance for practitioners" (second edition). London, UK: The Stationery Office. ISBN 978-0-11-331038-8

Index

Printed in the United States
by Baker & Taylor Publisher Services